Listening and Speaking

SKILLS FOR FIRST CERTIFICATE

Malcolm Mann
Steve Taylore-Knowles

MACMILLAN

Macmillan Education
Between Towns Road, Oxford OX4 3PP
A division of Macmillan Publishers Limited
Companies and representatives throughout the world

ISBN 1 405 01749 X

Text and design © Macmillan Publishers Limited 2003

First published 2003

All rights reserved; no part of this publication may be reproduced, stored in a retrieval system, or transmitted in any form or by any means, electronic, mechanical, photocopying, recording, or otherwise, without the prior written permission of the publishers.

Designed by Thomas Nicolaou at Polyplano, based on a design by Marc Thériault
Additional design by Anne Sherlock
Illustrated by Dimitris Kamenos
Cover design by Marc Thériault at Polyplano, Thessaloniki, Greece
Cover photo © PhotoDisc
Series editor: Emma Parker

Malcolm Mann would like to thank everyone at Macmillan for all their support and encouragement during the writing of this series.

Steve Taylore-Knowles would like to thank Jeanne, Sue, Emma, Yanni and George for making it happen and keeping it fun, Malc for putting up with putting him up, Jo for just putting up with him, and all his FC students whose faces and voices were constantly in his mind as he wrote.

The publishers would like to thank Ann Gibson, ELT Consultant. Thanks also to Jain Cook.

The authors and publishers would like to thank the following for permission to reproduce their photographs:
Corbis pp10, 14, 15, 16(tm), 22(tr), 28, 34, 35, 36(tl, tr), 38, 39, 40, 46, 50, 52, 58, 60, 62, 63, 70(tml, tmr, trr), 76, 82, 83, 86, 87, 88, 103; Photodisc p36 (br); Superstock pp16 (tr), 22(tml, tmr), 70(tl).

Commissioned Photography by Josephina Svania pp4, 64, 94

Printed and bound in Thailand

2007 2006 2005 2004
10 9 8 7 6 5 4 3 2

Contents

	Topic	Skills focus	Exam practice	Grammar focus	Page
1	Films	**Listening:** gist	**Listening Parts 1 & 2**	implied subjects	4
2	Occupations	**Speaking:** giving personal information	**Speaking Parts 1 & 2**	formal/informal	10
3	Education	**Listening:** identifying roles, relationships and location	**Listening Parts 3 & 4**	question tag intonation	16
4	Sport	**Speaking:** expressing attitude and opinion	**Speaking Parts 3 & 4**	one/any	22
5	People	**Listening:** understanding attitude and purpose	**Listening Parts 1 & 2**	infinitives of purpose	28
6	Travel	**Speaking:** comparing and contrasting	**Speaking Parts 1 & 2**	inversions with 'so'	34
7	Food and Drink	**Listening:** anticipating and predicting	**Listening Parts 3 & 4**	quite	40
8	The Media	**Speaking:** agreeing and disagreeing	**Speaking Parts 3 & 4**	prepositions with 'agree'	46
9	The Weather	**Listening:** note-taking and blank-filling	**Listening Parts 1 & 2**	elision in connected speech	52
10	The Environment	**Speaking:** speculating	**Speaking Parts 1 & 2**	deduction/obligation with 'must'	58
11	Technology	**Listening:** specific information	**Listening Parts 3 & 4**	verb/noun distinction	64
12	Health and Fitness	**Speaking:** discourse management	**Speaking Parts 3 & 4**	where/which + preposition	70
13	Transport	**Listening:** deducing meaning	**Listening Parts 1 & 2**	complete/incomplete action	76
14	Fashion	**Speaking:** pronunciation	**Speaking Parts 1 & 2**	transferred negative	82
15	Crime	**Listening:** understanding intonation and stress	**Listening Parts 3 & 4**	verb/noun stress	88
16	Shopping	**Speaking:** suggesting and recommending	**Speaking Parts 3 & 4**	what if/suppose	94

Exam know-how 100
Useful phrases 102
Speaking exam practice papers 103
Listening skills development 109

Unit 1 Films

WARM-UP *Pairwork*

Look at the pictures. In pairs, ask and answer the following questions:
- How often do you go to the cinema?
- Have you ever been to an outdoor cinema?
- How do outdoor cinemas differ from indoor cinemas?
- How could cinemas be improved to attract more people?

A

B

DEVELOP YOUR LISTENING SKILLS

A What's it like? *Pairwork*

Look at the following ways to see films. In pairs, talk about what it's like to see a film in this way. Try to mention at least one good point and one bad point.

Example:
'Well, I think watching a film on TV is great because you don't have to go to the cinema. You can watch it at home. But it's really annoying when there are lots of adverts in the middle of the film.'

on TV	on video	on DVD
at a local cinema	at an outdoor cinema	at a multi-screen cinema

similies. cinema — movies
— films
— "flicks"

cheap — inexpensive
dear — expensive / costly

B Listen and match
You are going to listen to five people talking about films. Match each speaker with the way they prefer to see a film. You will only use five of the ways.

Speaker 1 __F__   A TV — "the box". I'll watch anything. Don't like to choose.
Speaker 2 __B__   B video tapes. 'Pictures' = cinema = too costly. TV.
Speaker 3 __A__   C DVD p.c. disk. home entertainment. interactive. don't go to the movies
Speaker 4 __C__   D outdoor cinema "under the stars" — table. summer's evening anyone.
Speaker 5 __D__   E local (indoor) cinema
                   F multi-screen cinema — choice of movie "small screen"
                   comfort.
                   big screen.

C What did they say? (Pairwork)
Can you remember the reasons the speakers gave for their preferences? In pairs, make notes on the lines provided.

Speaker 1 _Close atmosphere on the TV. Sound and picture quality, choice of movies_
Speaker 2 _Large family → too expensive; more choices_
Speaker 3 _not good at making decisions_
Speaker 4 _tele digital and home cinema → control, choose own ending_
Speaker 5 _have table can eat & drink under the stars_

D Choose the best description
Now listen again. For each speaker, circle the sentence which best describes what they are saying.

Speaker 1
a The price must be cheap.
b The place must be right. atmosphere, Sound, Comfort.
c The film must be good.

Speaker 2
a We have to consider the time it takes.
b We have to consider how much choice we have.
c We have to consider the financial aspect. expense, cheap. costly,

Speaker 3
a I don't mind what I watch. anything.
b I don't mind where I watch it.
c I don't mind how I watch it.

Speaker 4
a Technology makes things quicker.
b Technology gives you more choice. control. interactive, choose ending
c Technology is becoming cheaper.

Speaker 5
a The film must be good. ✗
b Comfort is very important.
c I like the atmosphere. → special summer's evening.

Listening and Speaking Skills / Unit 1   5

Unit 1

DEVELOP YOUR LISTENING SKILLS

E *Were you right?*
Look again at the reasons you noted in C. Do you still agree with them? Make changes and additions to your notes where appropriate.

F *Discuss* (Pairwork)
As a class, discuss the reasons the five speakers gave for their preferences. Do you all agree?

G *Write some key words*
You're going to listen to the same five people. They will each be talking about a film they have just seen.
Before you listen, write down some key words you might expect to hear if someone is talking about the types of film below.

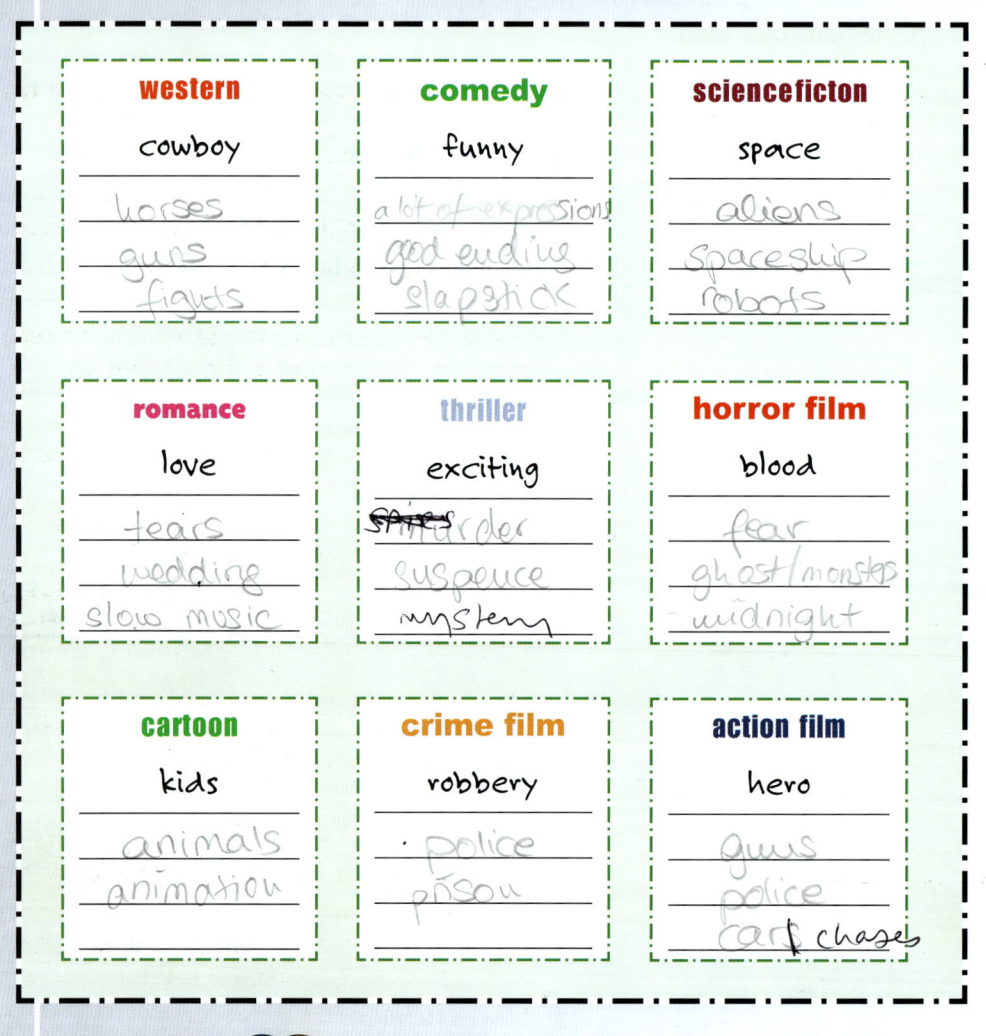

western	comedy	science ficton
cowboy	funny	space
horses	a lot of expressions	aliens
guns	good ending	spaceship
fights	slapstick	robots

romance	thriller	horror film
love	exciting	blood
tears	~~murder~~	fear
wedding	suspence	ghost/monsters
slow music	mystery	midnight

cartoon	crime film	action film
kids	robbery	hero
animals	· police	guns
animation	prison	police
		car chases

H *Discuss* (Pairwork)
Discuss your key words with the rest of the class. Did they think of any words that you didn't?

S⇔S what kind of film do you like most?

# Wordperfect

I Listen and circle
Now listen to the descriptions. As you listen, circle the type of film each speaker is describing.

Speaker 1
a comedy
b (science fiction) — robots, special effects, planetary

Speaker 2
a (cartoon) — toys; done by computer animation
b western — toy (cowboy)

Speaker 3
a crime film — (b) robbery, sentimental music
b (romance) — get together, split up

Speaker 4
a (action film) — cable car, car chases, jumping, edge of seat
b comedy — (b) fun

Speaker 5
a (horror film) — vampire, scary, aristocrat, Dracula, blood
b thriller

J Listen and circle
Now listen again. This time, decide if the statements are true or false. Circle **T** for True or **F** for False.

1 Speaker 1 thought the script was weak. plot, characterisation, comic re   T /(F)
2 Speaker 2 was impressed with the effects. animation, fantastic   (T)/ F
3 Speaker 3 really enjoyed the film. rubbish, boring   T /(F)
4 Speaker 4 had expected it to be better. actually, fun, "oh no"   T /(F)
5 Speaker 5 thought the ending was predictable. of course.   T / F

Read these sentences and then use the words in bold to complete the sentences below.

- It's not going to be a studio production. The whole movie is going to be filmed **on location** in the Alps.
- When people say they are going to '**the pictures**', they mean they are going to the cinema.
- It's a typical **western**. It's set in the Wild West in the late 1800s and it's about a group of cowboys who are attacked by some Indians.
- Terry Fisher and Barbara Walker are both film **critics**; they write film reviews for national newspapers.
- At the cinema, the short break in the middle of the film is sometimes called the **intermission**.
- A **film buff** is a person who likes films a lot, and knows a lot about them.
- I'd love to be a **stunt man**; it must be great fun doing all the dangerous stunts in a movie.
- Film **credits** at the end of a film tell us the names of the actors and the other people who were involved in the production of the film.
- If an actor has a **bit part** in a film, they only have a very small speaking role.
- If you are an **extra** in a movie, you can be seen in the background, but you don't have any lines to say.

1 I can't remember her name! We'll have to look at the ___credits___ at the end.
2 Most of the ___critics___ said it was a dreadful movie, but I really enjoyed it.
3 Making the movie was actually extremely hard, as we shot the whole thing ___on location___ in the desert.
4 Do you fancy going to ___the pictures___ tonight? I think that Jim Carrey comedy is still on.
5 Shall we get some popcorn during the ___intermission___?
6 Have you seen that ___western___ where Clint Eastwood plays a cowboy who hardly ever speaks?
7 Did you do the fight scenes yourself, or did a ___stunt man___ stand in for you?
8 I'd love to be an ___extra___, just to see what it's like on a film set.
9 Tom's a real ___film buff___; he'll know who directed *Night of the Living Dead*.
10 I've been offered a ___bit part___ in a movie! I'm only in one scene, but it's a start!

Listening and Speaking Skills / Unit 1   7"

Unit 1

EXAM PRACTICE — LISTENING PARTS 1 AND 2

Exam know-how

When you do Listening Part 1:
- As you read the questions, and hear them on the cassette, think about which key words you would expect to hear for each situation. Note down the key words you actually hear.

When you do Listening Part 2:
- Remember that the word or short phrase that you write will always be said on the cassette in exactly the same way. You will not need to change what you hear to fit the gap.

A Part 1

You will hear people talking in eight different situations. For questions **1-8**, choose the best answer, **A**, **B** or **C**.

1 You hear a woman being interviewed on the radio.
  What role did she have in a recent film?
  A an extra
  B a bit part
  C a main part

2 You overhear a woman in a video store. What does she want?
  A a film on video
  B a DVD
  C a blank video cassette

3 You overhear this exchange in a film on TV. What does the man want the woman to do?
  A press a button
  B pull a lever
  C turn a dial

4 You hear someone talking about a film. What kind of film is it?
  A a comedy
  B a western
  C a love story

5 Listen to this person talking about a film they worked on. What was their job?
  A actor
  B scriptwriter
  C director

6 You hear two people talking about a film. What is their relationship?
  A colleagues
  B neighbours
  C brothers

7 Listen to this woman on TV talking about a man. Why is she talking about him?
  A She's going to interview him.
  B She knows him personally.
  C He's a well-known actor.

8 Listen to this director talking to an actor. How does she want him to do the scene?
  A exactly as before
  B slightly differently
  C very differently

8

B Part 2

You will hear a radio interview with a stunt man. For questions **9-18**, complete the notes which summarise what the speaker says. You will need to write a word or short phrase in each box.

Actors don't always do all the [____ **9** ____] in a film.

Bill had to fight with [____ **10** ____] in his latest film.

Bill says that every job is [____ **11** ____]

Bill works for less than half the [____ **12** ____]

When Bill isn't working, he's with his [____ **13** ____]

[____ **14** ____] are not necessary to become a stunt man.

[____ **15** ____] are available for people thinking of doing stunt work.

Stunt men need to learn how to [____ **16** ____] properly.

Bill was a [____ **17** ____] before he became a stunt man.

The first film Bill worked on was about [____ **18** ____]

Grammar focus

We'd thought it was one of those spaghetti westerns from the 60s.
Turned out to be a ridiculous thing about a couple of struggling art students in New York.

The second sentence has no subject. It is implied.

What turned out to be a ridiculous thing? The film.

You will hear five people talking. Each person says two sentences.
For each speaker, circle the implied subject in the second sentence.

1 a the cinema   b the speaker
2 a the movie   b the speaker
3 a the DVD player   b Darren
4 a the movie   b the speaker
5 a Sindy   b Tom Hanks

Listening and Speaking Skills / Unit 1

Unit 2 Occupations

WARM-UP *Pairwork*

Look at the pictures. In pairs, play the Alphabet Job game:
Student A says a job beginning with 'a'. Student B says a job beginning with 'b', Student A says a job beginning with 'c', etc.

Which letters of the alphabet could you not find jobs for?

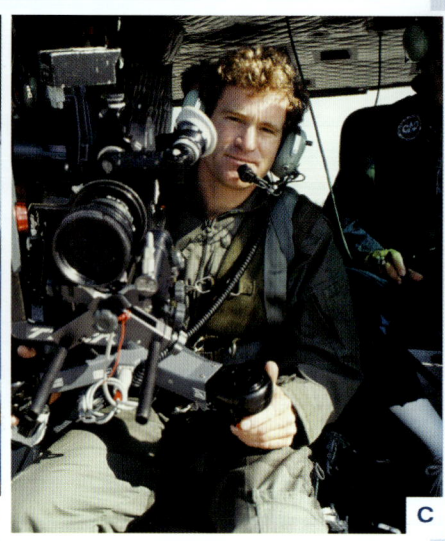

A B C

DEVELOP YOUR SPEAKING SKILLS

A *What might they ask?*

Look at this list of different topics. Which might you be asked about in Part 1 of the Speaking paper? Tick or cross.

1 your family ✓
2 your political views ✗
3 your hobbies and interests ✓
4 your plans for the future ✗
5 your secrets ✗
6 your local area ✓
7 your religious beliefs ✗
8 your present and future studies ✓

B Write questions

For each topic you ticked, write one short question you might be asked in Part 1 of the Speaking paper.

_____
_____
_____
_____
_____

C Dos and Don'ts

Which of these are good things for a candidate to say or do in Part 1? Which of them are not so good? Write **Do** or **Don't** before each one.

1 ✗ give one word answers.
2 ✓ give reasons for your opinions.
3 ✓ use contractions ('can't', 'won't', 'shouldn't', etc).
4 ✗ say 'My family consists of four members.'
5 ✓ say 'There are four of us in my family.'
6 ✗ say 'I live here for six years.'
7 ✓ say 'I've been living here for six years.'
8 ✗ say 'I go to a comprehensive/secondary school.'
9 ✗ say 'I will be a doctor.'
10 ✓ say 'I'd like to be a doctor.' or 'I want to be a doctor.'
11 ✗ just say 'I don't know' if you don't know what you want to do when you leave school.
12 ✓ say 'Well, I haven't really decided yet what I want to do when I leave school.'
13 ✗ say 'What?' if you didn't hear the question.
14 ✓ say 'Sorry, could you repeat the question?'

D Discuss *Pairwork*

In pairs, ask and answer the questions you wrote in B. Use the Dos and Don'ts above to help you.

Listening and Speaking Skills / Unit 2

Unit 2

DEVELOP YOUR SPEAKING SKILLS

E Listen and decide
You are going to hear some students being asked about jobs.
For each student, decide which question they are answering: a or b.

a What are you going to do when you leave school?
b Would you like to do the same job as your parents?

1 _b_ (No)
2 _a_
3 _a_
4 _a_
5 _b_ (No)
6 _b_ (No)
7 _a_
8 _b_ (No)

F Listen and circle
Now listen again. This time, decide whether the statements are true or false. Circle **T** for True or **F** for False.

1 Student 1 gives a reason for her opinion. **T / F**
2 Student 2 uses the word 'possibly'. **T / F**
3 Student 3 gives two reasons. **T / F**
4 Student 4 tells us what she wants to study at university. **T / F**
5 Student 5 tells us that both her parents work. **T / F**
6 Student 6 uses the second conditional to talk about a hypothetical situation. **T / F**
7 Student 7's voice goes up on her final word. **T / F**
8 Student 8 says 'I really believe …'. **T / F**

G Make notes
For each of these questions, make notes on the lines provided. Do not write full sentences. It doesn't matter if you put the same information into more than one box.

1 What are your plans for the future?

2 Have you decided on a career yet?

Wordperfect

3 What do you want to do when you leave school?

_____
_____
_____

4 Would you like to do the same job as your parents?

_____
_____
_____

5 Do you have either a full-time or a part-time job at the moment?

_____
_____
_____

H Discuss

As a class, ask and answer the questions in G. One student starts by asking another student one of the questions. When they have answered, it's their turn to ask another student one of the questions.

Read these sentences and then use the words in bold to complete the sentences below.

- I don't get a salary each month; I get 10% **commission** on every computer I sell.
- I sent off the **application form** for that job at the bank, and I've just heard they want me to come for an interview.
- Jobs which involve physical work are often described as **manual** jobs.
- People who do manual jobs are called 'manual workers' or '**blue collar workers**'.
- People who work in offices are sometimes called '**white collar workers**'.
- Adrian was given **the sack** when it was discovered he'd lied about his qualifications.
- Everyone in the office got a £200 **bonus** last Christmas. I hope we get one this year, too!
- People who work in government departments are called **civil servants**.
- When I was at university, I worked **part-time** in a newsagent's.
- If you say that a certain job or career is your **vocation**, you feel strongly that it's the right job or career for you.

1 You'll get _____ if you carry on being so late for work every day!
2 There's no _____; just send a C.V. and a covering letter to the Managing Director.
3 Anne's decided to go _____ now she's pregnant; she's only going to work two days a week.
4 I've always felt that it was my _____ to be a teacher. I've never wanted to do anything else.
5 The great thing about _____ is that the more you sell, the more money you make.
6 Is it true that Bruce Willis was a _____ worker in a factory before he became an actor?
7 Some _____ manage to work their way up the career ladder and become things like ambassadors and senior diplomats.
8 Many _____ have to make a real effort to stay fit; sitting at a desk all day is very unhealthy.
9 The _____ we give you will depend on how well you've done the job.
10 The closing of the factory led to 5,000 _____ being made redundant.

Listening and Speaking Skills / Unit 2 13

Unit 2

EXAM PRACTICE — SPEAKING PARTS 1 AND 2

Exam know-how

When you do Speaking Part 1:
- Remember that the truth is not very important. For example, if you can't remember the English word for the job you want to do, say a job that you do know in English.

When you do Speaking Part 2:
- Don't describe the photographs in detail. Think of each photo as an example of an idea. For example, if one photo is a picture of a nurse, it's the job you should talk about, not the particular nurse in the picture.

A Part 1

3 MIN

We'd like to know something about you, so I'm going to ask you some questions about yourselves.

- Where are you from?
- How do you usually spend your free time?
- Do you have either a full-time or a part-time job at the moment?
- What do your parents do?
- Have you decided on a career yet?
- What are your plans for the future?
- How ambitious are you?
- Would you like to do the same job as your parents?

B Part 2

1 MIN

Photos for Candidate A:

Candidate A, I'd like you to compare and contrast these pictures, saying how you would feel if you had these jobs.

Candidate B, which job would you prefer?

20 SECS

Photos for Candidate B:

> Candidate B, I'd like you to compare and contrast these pictures, saying which place you would prefer to work in.

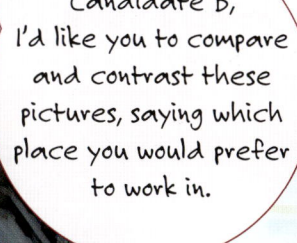

1 MIN

> Candidate A, how do you feel about these places?

20 SECS

Grammar focus

Formal written English:

I have not yet decided on a career.

Informal spoken English:

Well, I haven't really decided yet what I want to do.

Rewrite these sentences in the style of informal spoken English.

1 My father is currently unemployed and my mother works as an accountant.
   _____

2 I am considering becoming a vet as I greatly enjoy taking care of animals.
   _____

3 My main ambition is to establish my own small business.
   _____

4 I am not certain that I wish to go to university.
   _____

5 Job satisfaction is more important to me than a high salary.
   _____

Listening and Speaking Skills / Unit 2

Unit 3 Education

WARM-UP Pairwork

Look at the pictures. In pairs, discuss the following questions:
- What are the arguments in favour of school uniforms?
- What are the arguments against school uniforms?
- Do you think school uniforms are a good idea?
- Does it matter what teachers wear in the classroom?

A B C

DEVELOP YOUR LISTENING SKILLS

A Listen and match

Listen to the background noise from five different places. As you listen, match each noise with one of the places, **A-F**. You will only use five of the places.

1 E
2 B
3 A
4 F
5 C

A a playground
B a library
C a school canteen
D a car
E an office
F a shop

B What do you expect?

You're going to listen to seven people talking in different places. Before you listen, write down three things you might expect to hear them talking about in these places.

Example:			
at home	*TV*	*homework*	*meals*
in a classroom	_____	_____	_____
in a school staff room	_____	_____	_____
in a headteacher's office	_____	_____	_____
in a lecture hall	_____	_____	_____
in a car	_____	_____	_____
in a shop	_____	_____	_____

C Where are they?

Now listen to them talking.
As you listen, decide where the person is speaking.

Sammy.

1 _d_
2 _e_   *slide*
3 _c_   *essay mark*
4 _a_   *round Tommy's*
5 _g_   *in stock*
6 _b_   *turn to p.5.*
7 _f_   *turn left.*

a) at home
b) in a classroom
c) in a school staff room
d) in a headteacher's office
e) in a lecture hall
f) in a car
g) in a shop

Listening and Speaking Skills / Unit 3

Unit 3

DEVELOP YOUR LISTENING SKILLS

D Who's talking?

Now listen again. This time, write on the lines provided who you think is talking, and who they are talking to. Do not write any names.

Example:
Who is speaker 1?   headteacher
Who is speaker 1 talking to?   parent

2 Who is speaker 2?   _____
   Who is speaker 2 talking to?   _____

3 Who is speaker 3?   _____
   Who is speaker 3 talking to?   _____

4 Who is speaker 4?   _____
   Who is speaker 4 talking to?   _____

5 Who is speaker 5?   _____
   Who is speaker 5 talking to?   _____

6 Who is speaker 6?   _____
   Who is speaker 6 talking to?   _____

7 Who is speaker 7?   _____
   Who is speaker 7 talking to?   _____

E Listen and circle

Now listen to more of what they say.
For each statement below, circle the correct word.

1 The parent is worried / nervous.
2 The lecturer does / doesn't ask the audience a question.
3 The two teachers agree / disagree with each other.
4 The mother gives her son advice / permission.
5 The shop assistant is helpful / thoughtless.
6 The teacher is strict / rude.
7 The instructor is encouraging / critical.

Wordperfect

F What was it?

Look back at your answers to C, D and E. What do you think each situation is an example of? Circle the best choice.

Situation 1
a a meeting
b an interview

Situation 2
a a lesson
a a lecture

Situation 3
a a chat between friends
b a chat between colleagues

Situation 4
a a conversation
b a disagreement

Situation 5
a a conversation in a clothes shop
b a conversation in a shoe shop

Situation 6
a a meeting
b a lesson

Situation 7
a a driving test
b a driving lesson

G Discuss (Pairwork)

In pairs, discuss your answers to B, C, D and E. Do you agree on where they are? Do you agree on who is talking and who they are talking to? Did you circle the same words in E? Do you agree on what type of situation it is?

Read these sentences and then use the words in bold to complete the sentences below.

- I'm going to take a **gap year/year off/year out** before university, to travel round Europe.
- Our French **lesson** on Thursdays is two hours long.
- Physics is my least favourite **subject**. I find it so boring!
- If you are a **professor**, you have a very senior position in a department at a university.
- A **lecturer** is a teacher at a university or college. He/She is less senior than a professor.
- When I was at university, I had ten hours of **lectures** and six hours of seminars each week.
- Melissa is an **undergraduate** at Warwick University. If she passes her exams, she'll get her degree next summer.
- I got my degree in English Literature, then I did an MA and now I'm working for my **PhD**. When I get that, I'll officially be called Doctor Stephens.
- Pauline teaches kids with **special needs** at a Comprehensive in London. She says it's hard work, but very rewarding.
- When I was at school, the **school uniform** was a pair of grey trousers and a blue sweater. We wore grey shorts in the summer!

1 Teachers have begun to realise that learners with _____, such as children with dyslexia, need particular help and support.
2 Dr Dawkins' _____ are always entertaining. He makes astrophysics come alive.
3 Wearing a _____ means you don't have to worry about what to put on!
4 I went to Australia for my _____. It taught me about surviving in the real world.
5 There was a fire practice during our German _____ this morning, so we didn't have a test!
6 Simon was a/an _____ for twenty years before they made him a professor.
7 When I was a/an _____, you used to get a grant from the government to cover your living expenses at university.
8 I'm thinking of doing a _____ on the similarities between Eminem's rap lyrics and the poetry of Robert Browning.
9 Like most university lecturers, Angela hopes to become a _____ one day.
10 I'm thinking of doing another A level, but I can't decide which _____ to choose.

Listening and Speaking Skills / Unit 3 19

Unit 3

EXAM PRACTICE — LISTENING PARTS 3 AND 4

Exam know-how

When you do Listening Part 3:
- They don't say 'Speaker One', 'Speaker Two', etc between the extracts; there is just a short pause. For this reason, if you're not sure of the answer, it's a good idea to put a mark or a tick next to the box. This will stop you writing the answer for the next question in the wrong box.

When you do Listening Part 4:
- There is a variety of different exercise types in this part. You might be asked to answer True or False questions, Yes or No questions, three-option multiple choice questions, or even 'Which speaker said what?' questions. For this reason, it is extremely important to read and listen to the instructions carefully.

A Part 3

You will hear five people talking about teachers they had when they were at school. For questions **1-5**, choose from the list **A-F** how each one of them describes his or her teacher. Use the letters only once. There is one extra letter you do not need to use.

A He/She was encouraging.

Speaker 1 [C] 1

B He/She was sympathetic.

Speaker 2 [F] 2

C He/She was funny.

Speaker 3 [B] 3

D He/She was strict.

Speaker 4 [A] 4

E He/She was generous.

Speaker 5 [E] 5

F He/She was respectful.

Part 4

You will hear a conversation which takes place in a seminar at university, between a lecturer and two students, Erika and Paul. Answer questions **6-12** by writing

- **L** for **Lecturer**
- **E** for **Erika**
- or **P** for **Paul**, in the boxes provided.

Sorry guys

6	Who apologises for being late?	*I was working over the summer*	**L**	6	*staff meeting*
7	Who explains that they were <u>too busy</u> to do something? *read.*		**E**	7	
8	Who wants to consider more than one book? *comparing 2 texts..*		**P**	8	
9	Who rejects someone's suggestion? *I'd rather you didn't*		**L**	9	
10	Who mentions being a student? *I did sth similar when undergraduate*		**L**	10	
11	Who thought the deadline was later? *I thought we had until 30th*		**E**	11	
12	Who is going away on a trip? — *I'll be away on that s/same week.*		**P**	12	

Grammar focus

Listen to someone saying this sentence two different ways:

You didn't go to Cambridge, did you?

↗ *wants answer*
↘ *wants confirmation — knows the answer.*

The meaning depends on the tone of voice.
The first time, the speaker expects the answer 'No, I didn't.'
The second time, another person has just said that they went to Cambridge, and the speaker is expressing surprise at this information.

Now listen to these seven questions. For each one, decide if the speaker expects the answer 'No', or if they are surprised at the information they have just heard. Tick the appropriate box.

	expects 'No'	surprised
1	☐	✓ ↗
2	☐	✓ ↗
3	✓	☐ ↘
4	☐	✓ ↗
5	✓	☐ ↘
6	✓	☐ ↘
7	☐	✓ ↗

Unit 4 Sport

WARM-UP *Pairwork*

Look at the pictures. Do you know what these things are?
In pairs, write down as many different pieces of sporting equipment as you can.
You have three minutes.
How many could you think of?

A   B   C   D

DEVELOP YOUR SPEAKING SKILLS

A Dos and Don'ts

Which of these are good things for a candidate to say or do in Speaking Part 3? Which of them are not so good? Write **Do** or **Don't** before each one.

1 _____ talk to the interviewer.
2 _____ talk to the other candidate.
3 _____ always agree with the other candidate.
4 _____ give reasons for your opinions.
5 _____ use words like 'maybe', 'perhaps', 'possibly'.
6 _____ use words like 'would', 'could', 'should', 'may', 'might'.
7 _____ worry if you don't finish the whole task in three minutes.

B Part 3 or Part 4?

You are going to hear some students talking about sport in the Speaking paper. For each student, decide if they are doing Part 3 or Part 4 of the paper. Write **3** or **4** on the line provided.

Student 1 _____   Student 5 _____
Student 2 _____   Student 6 _____
Student 3 _____   Student 7 _____
Student 4 _____

C Listen and answer

Now listen to the students again. As you listen, write answers to the questions on the lines provided.

1 Which word does Student 1 use to introduce a reason? _____
2 Which word does Student 2 use to mean 'also'? _____
3 Which phrase does Student 3 use to tell us this is the first reason? _____
4 Which word does Student 4 use to introduce a result? _____
5 Which conditional does Student 5 use (1st, 2nd or 3rd)? _____
6 Which phrase does Student 6 use to show that something is a good choice? _____
7 Which word does Student 7 use to show a second possibility? _____

D Discuss (Pairwork)

Do you agree on the parts?
Did you write down the same answers for C?

E What are they used for?

Here are some words and phrases students often use in Speaking Parts 3 and 4. What are they for? Write them in the correct boxes.

A As far as I'm concerned, ...
A I think that ...
   ... too.
   ... so ...
   ... also ...

D Apart from that, ...
   ... as ...
   Because of this, ...
A Personally, ...
   Take ...

   ... because ...
   ..., such as ...
   ... as well.
   I don't think that ...
   It seems to me that ...

A Expressing opinion

D Giving a further reason

E Introducing reasons

B Giving examples

E Introducing results

Unit 4

DEVELOP YOUR SPEAKING SKILLS

F *Look and complete the table*
Look at this Speaking Part 3 task and make notes to complete the table opposite.

I'd like you to imagine that a friend of yours called Angela, who is a teenager, wants to take up a new sport. She wants to get fit, have fun and make new friends. She has asked for your advice. Here are some possible sports.

1
2
3
4
5

I'd like you to talk to each other and discuss where in your area she could do these activities. Then, I'd like you to decide which sport you would recommend, and why.

3 MIN

Wordperfect

1	Name of sport	_____
	Can do in local area?	Yes/No/Not sure
	If yes, where?	_____
	Recommend?	Yes/No
	Why/Why not?	_____
2	Name of sport	_____
	Can do in local area?	Yes/No/Not sure
	If yes, where?	_____
	Recommend?	Yes/No
	Why/Why not?	_____
3	Name of sport	_____
	Can do in local area?	Yes/No/Not sure
	If yes, where?	_____
	Recommend?	Yes/No
	Why/Why not?	_____
4	Name of sport	_____
	Can do in local area?	Yes/No/Not sure
	If yes, where?	_____
	Recommend?	Yes/No
	Why/Why not?	_____
5	Name of sport	_____
	Can do in local area?	Yes/No/Not sure
	If yes, where?	_____
	Recommend?	Yes/No
	Why/Why not?	_____

G Do the task

In pairs, do the Speaking Part 3 task.
- Remember there are two parts to the task.
- The first part is to talk to each other and discuss where in your area she could do these activities. This should take about one and a half minutes.
- The second part is to to decide which sport you would recommend, and why. This should take about one and a half minutes.
- Use your notes in the table to help you.
- Try to use some of the words and phrases from E.
- Look again at the Dos and Don'ts in A before you start.

Read these sentences and then use the words in bold to complete the sentences below.

- The hotel is situated close to a professional 18-hole **golf course.**
- Have you ever done any **extreme sports** like parachuting or hang-gliding?
- Let's have a look at the **action replay** to see the goal again in slow motion.
- Mum, is my sports **kit** clean? I've got a match this afternoon.
- Dave can't wait until Saturday. It's the **final** of the European Cup.
- Manchester United **beat** Coventry City last night.
- Cricket and tennis don't have referees; they have **umpires**.
- There are two types of event in athletics: **track** events and field events.
- I love **motor racing**. It's my favourite sport. I never miss the Grand Prix when it's on TV.
- I'm not very keen on **team games**; I prefer sports where there are only two players competing against each other.

1 Two _____ are needed for a cricket match, but only one for a tennis match.
2 Baseball, water-polo and volleyball are all examples of _____.
3 Now you're in the team, we'll have to get you a new _____. You'll need a shirt, shorts and some football boots, won't you?
4 Apparently, it's the most difficult _____ in the country. Even professional players have problems getting the ball across the lake near the 13th hole.
5 I hated running the 1500m. You had to go round the _____ so many times. It was so boring!
6 _____ is getting too dangerous. Two Formula 1 drivers were killed last year.
7 Who's playing in the _____? Is it France against Germany?
8 If you look at the _____, you'll see that the goalkeeper just touched the ball with his hand as it went in the net.
9 More and more young people are taking up _____ such as snowboarding and bungee-jumping.
10 If England don't _____ Poland on Tuesday, then they're out of the Championship.

Listening and Speaking Skills / Unit 4

Unit 4

EXAM PRACTICE — SPEAKING PARTS 3 AND 4

Exam know-how

When you do Speaking Part 3:
- You should only speak to the other candidate. Don't talk to the examiner at all. Imagine that he/she is not there.

When you do Speaking Part 4:
- You will mainly be answering the examiner's questions, but feel free to agree/disagree with what the other candidate says. You will impress the examiner if you talk directly to the other candidate.

A Part 3

I'd like you to imagine that you are best friends. You are on an adventure holiday, and tomorrow is your final day. You have a choice of activities. You haven't done any of them yet on the holiday and you want to do one of them together tomorrow. Here are the choices.

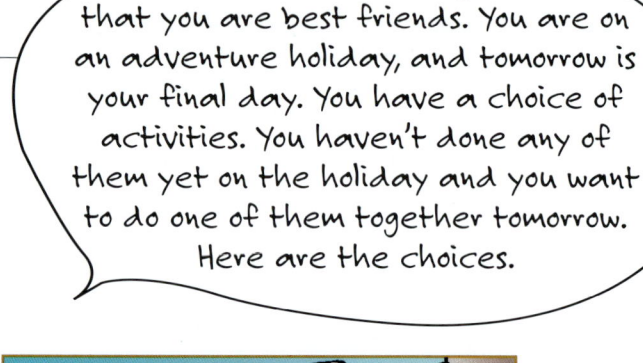

I'd like you to talk to each other and discuss how enjoyable you think these activities would be. Then, I'd like you to decide which activity you're going to do tomorrow, and why. Remember, you have about three minutes for this.

3 MIN

B Part 4

- What's your favourite sport? Why?
- Have you ever been on an adventure holiday?
- Would you describe yourself as a sporty person?
- Are you in any teams?
- Would you like to try any extreme sports? Which ones? Why?
- What is more important: winning or taking part?
- Do you think children should have to do P.E. at school? Why/Why not?
- How important is sport to you?

Grammar focus

I've got to buy a tennis racket as I haven't got **one**. (singular countable noun)
I've got to buy some tennis balls as I haven't got **any**. (plural countable noun)
I've got to buy some fishing tackle as I haven't got **any**. (uncountable noun)

Write 'one' or 'any' in the gaps to complete the sentences.

1 I wanted to get some new weightlifting equipment from the sports shop, but they didn't have _____.
2 Anna wanted to go to an ice-skating rink but it seems there isn't _____ near here.
3 I tried to get some tickets for the match on Saturday, but there aren't _____ left.
4 He said he'd do lots of training, but in fact he hasn't done _____!
5 Apparently, you need a licence to fish there, and Alan didn't have _____.

Listening and Speaking Skills / Unit 4

Unit 5 People

WARM-UP Pairwork

Look at the pictures. In pairs, do the following tasks and answer the question:
- Quickly write down as many words as you can to describe how the people in these photographs feel.
- Write one sentence you think they might be thinking at this moment.
- How do the photographs make you feel?

A   B   C

DEVELOP YOUR LISTENING SKILLS

A How do they feel?

Four people were asked about a famous performer. Listen to these short extracts from what they said. For each speaker, choose the adjective which best describes how they feel.

Speaker 1
a impressed
b shocked
c bored

Speaker 2
a amused
b annoyed
c disappointed

Speaker 3
a jealous
b upset
c excited

Speaker 4
a surprised
b grateful
c worried

B   What do they think about her?

Now listen to the complete responses. For each speaker, choose the sentence which best describes their attitude towards the famous person. There is one extra sentence you do not need to use.

Speaker 1 _____   A I don't think people give her a chance.
Speaker 2 _____   B I think anybody could have done the same. 3
Speaker 3 _____   C I understand now why people like her. 1
Speaker 4 _____   D I think she's helped other people. 4
                            E I don't like the way she's changed. 2

C   Guess the emotion   *Pairwork*

Read the following sentences to each other. Use one of the tones of voice from the box. Try to guess which emotion your partner is expressing and then repeat the sentence using another tone of voice.

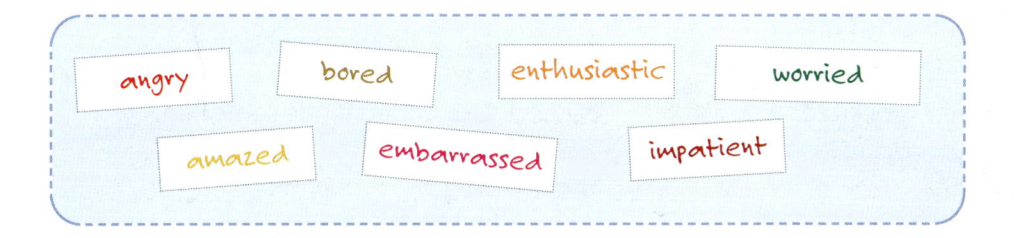

> angry   bored   enthusiastic   worried
> amazed   embarrassed   impatient

'I don't like to be with too many people.'

'There's a man in our town who says he's 110 years old.'

'The population of the world is over six billion.'

'I invited fifty people to my party, and only five turned up.'

Listening and Speaking Skills / Unit 5

Unit 5

DEVELOP YOUR LISTENING SKILLS

D Think about it

You are going to hear messages left on an answering machine.
Tick the information people normally include in their messages.

In their messages, people normally include ...

1 their name. _____
2 their age. _____
3 the day. _____
4 the time. _____
5 the month. _____
6 the reason they're calling. _____

E Why did they call?

Listen to these messages left on a woman's answering machine.
For each speaker, circle the reason they called.

Speaker 1
He is calling to find out whether ...
a Lisa got a message.
b Lisa is still working.
c the party has been cancelled.

Speaker 2
She is calling to tell Lisa about ...
a her evening out.
b a change in plans.
c her wasted day.

Speaker 3
She is calling to ...
a remind Lisa about something.
b ask Lisa to come later.
c check Lisa understands something.

Speaker 4
He is calling to ask Lisa for ...
a permission.
b advice.
c information.

F Listen and circle

Listen again. This time, circle which of the following phrases each speaker uses to introduce their reason for calling.

Speaker 1
a I merely wanted to ...
b I really wanted to ...

Speaker 2
a One thing is that ...
b The thing is that ...

Speaker 3
a The reason for calling is ...
b The reason I'm calling is ...

Speaker 4
a To cut to the point, ...
b To get to the point, ...

Wordperfect

G How does Lisa feel?
Listen to this conversation between Lisa and her friend about the messages left on the answering machine. For each subject, circle how Lisa feels about it.

1 Lisa feels _____ about Greg not coming to the party.
   a annoyed
   b relieved
   c anxious

2 Lisa feels _____ Maria's trip to America.
   a excited about
   b jealous of
   c nervous about

3 Lisa feels _____ the call from the hairdresser's.
   a upset by
   b grateful for
   c angry about

4 Lisa feels _____ by Mark's phone call.
   a amused
   b worried
   c deceived

H True or false?
Listen again and decide whether the following statements are true or false. Circle **T** for True or **F** for False.

1 Lisa was pleased with the restaurant they went to.   T / F

2 Greg arrived late at Lisa's last party.   T / F

3 This is probably Maria's last chance to go to America.   T / F

4 Lisa told the hairdresser that the assistant was very rude.   T / F

5 Lisa is worried that she might be losing her memory.   T / F

Read these sentences and then use the words in bold to complete the sentences below.

- I relied on John and he really **let** me **down**; I was so disappointed.
- When people are **upset**, they feel sad and perhaps cry.
- My **social life** has got much better since I moved to the city and I've met lots of new people.
- The **population** of Japan is nearly 130 million.
- If something is **inconvenient**, it causes you trouble by happening at the wrong time or place.
- You feel **relieved** when you stop worrying about something.
- You might feel **anxious** when you are a little afraid or when you are worrying about something.
- You should show how **grateful** you are and say 'Thank you' when you receive a gift.
- The reason you are doing something is your **purpose**.
- The headmaster was **furious** when he saw the broken window and shouted at all of us.

1 Nancy's parents were very _____ when the police found her safe.
2 If it's not too _____, maybe we could meet outside the library at seven.
3 My mum was absolutely _____ when she heard that I'd been fighting at school.
4 Louise was really _____ by some of the horrible things you said and she was in tears all night.
5 I'm so sorry to _____ you _____, but I can't help you this weekend after all.
6 If the _____ of the world continues to increase, what problems do you think we will face in the future?
7 Ian has quite a full _____ and always seems to be going out with friends.
8 I can't tell you how _____ I am for all the wonderful Christmas presents.
9 I'm a bit _____ about the exam tomorrow because it's quite important.
10 I really couldn't understand what the _____ of doing so many grammar exercises was when we all knew how to do it.

Listening and Speaking Skills / Unit 5

Unit 5

EXAM PRACTICE — LISTENING PARTS 1 AND 2

Exam know-how

When you do Listening Part 2:
- If you aren't sure you understand what a speaker is saying, listen to their tone of voice. You can often tell how somebody feels by the tone they use.
- It's possible that an answer is a number, such as somebody's age or even a telephone number. Remember that you don't have to write the answer in letters and can just write the number in figures if you want to.

A Part 1

You will hear people talking in eight different situations. For questions **1-8**, choose the best answer, **A**, **B** or **C**.

1 You overhear this exchange in an office. How does the man feel?
   A relieved
   B embarrassed
   C disappointed

2 You hear a woman talking about a party. What did she feel about the man she met?
   A He was helpful.
   B He was funny.
   C He was powerful.

3 Listen to this man talking to someone on the phone. Why is he calling?
   A to rearrange a meeting
   B to cancel a meeting
   C to report on a meeting

4 You hear this woman talking on a radio show. Why did she call?
   A to request a song
   B to enter a competition
   C to give her opinion

5 In a shop, you hear an assistant on the phone. How does she feel?
   A annoyed with her manager
   B upset with a customer
   C worried about a delivery

6 You overhear this conversation on a bus. What does the woman want her husband to do?
   A mend the car
   B clean the car
   C sell the car

7 You hear this man describing a book. What is his attitude towards it?
   A It had a great effect on him.
   B It didn't teach him anything new.
   C It made him feel guilty.

8 Listen to this woman talking to her son. What does she want him to do?
   A write a letter
   B make a phone call
   C visit someone

B Part 2

You will hear part of a radio programme about a famous person. For questions **9-18**, complete the notes which summarise what the speaker says. You will need to write a word or short phrase in each box.

The [_____ **9** _____] were all surprised by her wedding.

Her first part was in a [_____ **10** _____]

As a child, she wanted to be [_____ **11** _____]

Denise learnt more about the theatre when she [_____ **12** _____]

She met Peter Jones at [_____ **13** _____]

They spent some time living in [_____ **14** _____] together in Hollywood.

Peter worked hard to get [_____ **15** _____] interested in his ideas.

To make money, Denise worked in [_____ **16** _____]

Andy Foster was impressed by the [_____ **17** _____] Peter showed him.

They started making *My Previous Life* [_____ **18** _____] after Andy met Denise.

Grammar focus

Look at the following statements using the infinitive:

To make my mum happy, I called my grandma.
To tell you the truth, I didn't want to call my grandma.

The first expresses a purpose and tells us why the speaker did something. It is the same as saying:

I called my grandma in order to make my mum happy.

The second is a linking phrase and does not express a purpose. It is the same as saying:

Really, I didn't want to call my grandma.

Listen to these people making statements using infinitives.
Decide if they are using infinitives of purpose by circling the correct answer.

Speaker 1
a expressing a purpose
b not expressing a purpose

Speaker 2
a expressing a purpose
b not expressing a purpose

Speaker 3
a expressing a purpose
b not expressing a purpose

Speaker 4
a expressing a purpose
b not expressing a purpose

Speaker 5
a expressing a purpose
b not expressing a purpose

Speaker 6
a expressing a purpose
b not expressing a purpose

Listening and Speaking Skills / Unit 5

Unit 6 Travel

WARM-UP *Pairwork*

Look at the pictures. In pairs, decide whether you agree or disagree with the following statements and explain why.

- Camping is really uncomfortable and I prefer to stay in a hotel on holiday.
- A holiday is a chance to do new activities and try out new hobbies.
- My idea of a holiday is lying on the beach with friends.

A   B   C

DEVELOP YOUR SPEAKING SKILLS

A Dos and Don'ts

Which of these are good things for you to say or do in Part 2? Which of them are not so good? Write **Do** or **Don't** before each one.

1 _____ describe the photographs in as much detail as you can.
2 _____ compare and contrast the photographs.
3 _____ mention the main similarities between the photographs.
4 _____ mention the main differences between the photographs.
5 _____ worry if the examiner interrupts you after a minute.
6 _____ listen when your partner is talking.
7 _____ listen to exactly what question the examiner asks you.
8 _____ stop after thirty seconds and say 'That's all.'
9 _____ get stuck trying to think of one word.
10 _____ think of a different way of saying something if you forget a word.

B Listen and choose

Listen to this student comparing and contrasting two pictures of holidays. Decide which two pictures she is talking about and tick the points she makes. Listen again if necessary.

She is talking about picture __A__ and picture __B__.

She says that ...
1 they are both challenging holiday activities. ✓
2 they are both done at the same time of year. ✓
3 the photos were taken in different places. ✓
4 different people prefer different activities. ___
5 she finds one activity more exciting. ✓

C Match to make sentences

Here are some other points about the photographs the student could have made, using the linking phrases in bold. Match the two halves of the sentences.

1 Canoeing could be dangerous, __d__
2 **In contrast to** cycling, __c__
3 Canoeing is rather unusual, __a__
4 Cycling can be tiring on holiday, __e__
5 You need special equipment to go canoeing, __b__

a **unlike** cycling, which some people do everyday.
b **while** for cycling you don't.
c canoeing demands special training.
d **whereas** cycling is usually quite safe.
e and so can canoeing.

Unit 6

DEVELOP YOUR SPEAKING SKILLS

D *Discuss* — Pairwork

Look at these two pictures of different kinds of holiday. With your partner, decide what you think are the two most important similarities and the two most important differences. Write them in the box. Then discuss your ideas with the class.

A

B

Similarities

1 _____

2 _____

Differences

1 _____

2 _____

E *Complete the text*

This person is talking about the pictures above. Complete what is said using the useful phrases below. Write the correct letters in the spaces provided.

(1) _c_, both photographs show holidays. (2) _g_ people on a beach, (3) _a_ the second is of people riding an elephant.
(4) _e_, the people seem to be relaxed because they are taking a break from work. The photo of the beach was probably taken in the summer (5) _h_ was the other one. (6) _d_ spending your holiday lying on a beach can be a little boring, (7) ____ exotic holidays, which teach you about other countries and other people. (8) ____ beach holidays, exotic holidays are (9) ____ interesting.

a while/whereas
b Compared with
c To begin with
d One main difference is that
e In both pictures
f in contrast to
g The first is a photograph of
h and so
i more

36

Wordperfect

F **Compare and contrast**
Look at the photographs again with your partner and practise comparing and contrasting using the useful phrases in E. One of you should read the examiner's words and then listen. When you have finished, swap roles and practise again.

Here are two pictures of holidays. I'd like you to compare and contrast them and tell us which kind of holiday you would prefer. Remember, you only have one minute.

G **What could you say?**
Imagine you had photographs of the following things. What is the most important similarity you might mention? What is the most important difference? Work with your partner, and then discuss your ideas with the class.

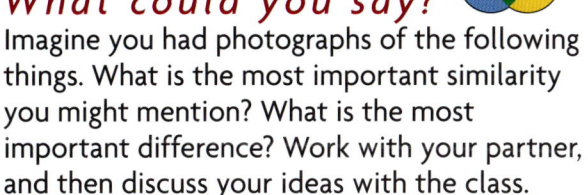

1 a train/an aeroplane

Example:
They are both fast means of transport, but we usually use aeroplanes for longer distances.

2 a camping holiday/a beach holiday
3 a trip to London/a trip to Moscow
4 a luxury hotel/a cheap hotel

Read these sentences and then use the words in bold to complete the sentences below.

- When you arrive in another country, you have to go through **customs**, where they check you don't have anything illegal.
- Shops at airports often sell **duty free** products, which means they are much cheaper because you don't pay any tax.
- For some places you need a **visa**, which gives you permission to enter the country.
- The road is blocked so we'll have to find a different **route** to the hotel.
- Make sure you have everything you need before you **set off** on your journey.
- Many children learn a lot by going away to **summer camp** with their friends.
- A **charter** flight is usually cheap and takes tourists in the summer.
- A **scheduled** flight goes all year and is usually more expensive.
- On a **self-catering holiday**, you stay in rooms and cook your own meals.
- I would love to go on an **adventure holiday** and try activities like canoeing.

1 I'm waiting for my _____ so that I can visit Australia.
2 I had a great time at _____ and made lots of new friends my own age.
3 The _____ flight to Barcelona leaves at 9.00 every day, all year round.
4 My mum asked me to get her some _____ perfume when I go to America.
5 On a walking holiday, it's a good idea to mark your _____ on the map so you don't get lost.
6 We're going to Spain in July so there should be lots of cheap _____ flights.
7 We had only just _____ when I realised I hadn't locked the door and we had to go back.
8 I'd love to hear about the _____ you went on. How did you like rock climbing and canoeing?
9 Mrs Wilson was stopped at _____ and they looked through all her luggage.
10 We couldn't afford to stay in a hotel, so we decided to go on a _____ in France.

Listening and Speaking Skills / Unit 6

Unit 6

Exam practice — speaking parts 1 and 2

Exam know-how

When you do Speaking Part 2:
- You will always be asked to compare and contrast two photographs. The examiner will also ask you to express an opinion. Often, you are asked to say which you prefer, but you might be asked to talk about something else. Listen to the question and make sure you answer the question you have been asked.
- Remember that you only have one minute to talk about the two photographs. Don't spend too long talking about one of them. Don't worry if the examiner interrupts you after a minute — it just means you have a lot of ideas!

A Part 1

3 min

We'd like to know something about you, so I'm going to ask you some questions about yourselves.

- Do you like to be active when you are on holiday?
- Have you travelled much?
- What can tourists do in your area?
- Would you rather go on holiday with your family or with friends?
- Where would you like to go on holiday if you had the chance?
- Have you ever been camping?
- Have you ever been abroad?
- Where did you go for your last holiday? Did you enjoy it?

B Part 2

1 min

Photos for Candidate A:

Candidate A, here are two photographs of different kinds of holiday. I'd like you to compare and contrast them and say how you feel about holidays like these. Remember, you only have one minute.

Candidate B, which holiday would you prefer?

20 secs

Photos for Candidate B:

Candidate B, here are two photographs of different places to stay on holiday. I'd like you to compare and contrast them and tell us which place you would prefer to stay in. Remember, you only have one minute.

1 MIN

Candidate A, have you ever stayed in places like these?

20 SECS

Grammar *focus*

Look at these sentences using 'so' to make a comparison. Notice the word order and which auxiliary verbs are used.

Flying is quite safe, and **so** is travelling by train.
The people in the first photograph have been travelling, and **so** have those in the second.
Adventure holidays can be dangerous, and **so** can swimming in some areas.
The people in the first photograph seem excited, and **so** do those in the second.

Use 'so' and an appropriate auxiliary verb to complete the following sentences.

1 My father has visited many European countries, and _____ I.
2 The first photo was taken outdoors, and _____ the second.
3 Travelling by plane can be exciting, and _____ travelling by ship.
4 Many people are afraid of flying, and _____ I.
5 Many people like beach holidays, and _____ I.
6 The first photo looks interesting, and _____ the second.

Listening   and   Speaking   Skills / Unit 6   39

Unit 7

Food and Drink

WARM-UP *Pairwork*

Look at the pictures. In pairs, discuss whether you agree or disagree with the following statements. Explain why.
- I really don't like foreign food and the idea of it makes me feel sick.
- I love spicy food. The hotter, the better!
- I like to taste new and unusual food. I'll try anything once.
- I think everybody likes the kind of food they grow up with.

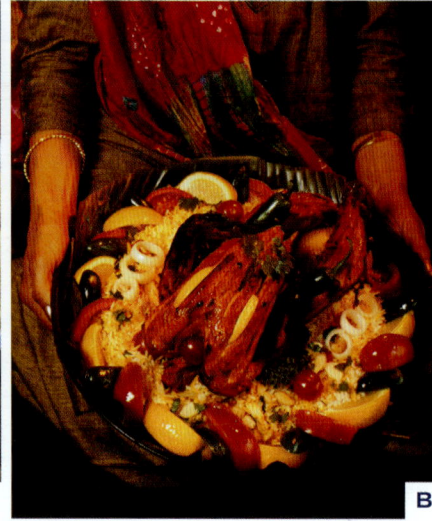

A   B   C

DEVELOP YOUR LISTENING SKILLS

A   What are they going to say?

You are going to listen to some people talking about the cuisine of different countries. First, listen to one sentence from each person and predict what they are going to talk about next by choosing the correct answer.

Speaker 1 is going to talk about
a   some of the ingredients of Indian food.
b   some of his experiences in Indian restaurants.

Speaker 2 is going to talk about
a   the history of Italian food.
b   the image of Italian food.

Speaker 3 is going to talk about
a   some problems with Chinese food.
b   some misunderstandings about Chinese food.

Speaker 4 is going to talk about
a some less well-known English dishes.
b some health dangers of the English diet.

Speaker 5 is going to talk about
a how people in Mexico make a particular dish.
b what a particular Mexican dish tastes like.

B Listen and check
Listen to what the speakers said next and check your answers to A.

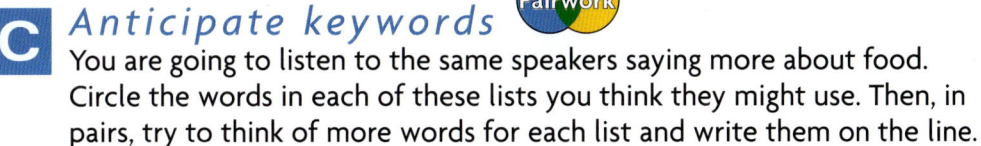

C Anticipate keywords
You are going to listen to the same speakers saying more about food. Circle the words in each of these lists you think they might use. Then, in pairs, try to think of more words for each list and write them on the line.

Speaker 1: Indian food
spicy chips popular hot popcorn vegetables
_____

Speaker 2: Italian food
tomatoes pizza chopsticks restaurants chocolate cheese
_____

Speaker 3: Chinese food
healthy microwave steak rice crisps fried
_____

Speaker 4: English food
stew octopus potatoes Mediterranean tasty traditions
_____

Speaker 5: Mexican food
rice vodka chillies chicken pizza burgers
_____

D Listen and check
Listen to the complete recordings and check which keywords from C the speakers actually used. Did they use any of your words?

Listening and Speaking Skills / Unit 7   41

Unit 7

DEVELOP YOUR LISTENING SKILLS

E Listen and match

Listen to the speakers again and choose which of the following ideas each speaker expresses by writing the correct letter in the space provided. There is one extra letter you do not need to use.

Speaker 1 _____
Speaker 2 _____
Speaker 3 _____
Speaker 4 _____
Speaker 5 _____

A This food shows that we should try to find out more.
B This food is thought to be better home-made.
C This food is appropriate in the country it comes from.
D This food doesn't demand a lot of preparation time.
E This food is done better in the country it comes from.
F This food appeals to all kinds of different people.

F What are the missing words?

You are going to listen to an extract from an interview with the speaker you heard talking about Indian food. Before you listen, try to predict what words are missing from these notes by circling the correct answer and then writing your guess on the line provided.

1 He thought before he went that people ate more _____ than they actually did.

   The missing word is probably ...
   a a noun.
   b an adjective.
   c a verb.

   It could be: _____

2 Some of the food is quite _____ for local people.

   The missing word is probably ...
   a an adverb.
   b a preposition.
   c an adjective.

   It could be: _____

3 If the food was too _____, the speaker didn't like it.

   The missing word is probably ...
   a an adjective.
   b a verb.
   c a noun.

   It could be: _____

42

Wordperfect

G Discuss *Pairwork*
In pairs, discuss your ideas. Do you agree on what the missing words might be?

H Are these possible?
Decide whether the following words could be used to complete any of the sentences 1-3 in F. Write the number(s) of the sentences next to the words. If the word can't be used to complete any of the sentences, put a cross.

1 cheap   _____
2 quickly   _____
3 rather   _____
4 potatoes   _____
5 curry   _____
6 salty   _____

I Listen and complete
Listen to the extract from the interview and complete the notes in F. Were any of your guesses correct?

J Listen and circle
Now listen again. This time, decide if the statements are true or false. Circle **T** for True or **F** for False.

1 The speaker did some research before he went.   **T / F**
2 The speaker was expecting more vegetables.   **T / F**
3 The Indians eat a large amount of beef.   **T / F**
4 The speaker loved everything he ate.   **T / F**

Read these sentences and then use the words in bold to complete the sentences below.

- I've always loved French **cuisine** and I took a course to learn how to cook it properly.
- This one's quite **spicy**, so you might need a glass of water with it to cool your mouth down!
- In Europe, we eat quite well but we still have too much salt and sugar in our **diet**.
- A person who makes food but who hasn't been specially trained is usually called a **cook**.
- Some places are **self-service** and don't have waiters. You get your food from the counter and pay for it before sitting at a table.
- If you **acquire/get a taste for** something, you try it and start to like it.
- The waiter told us that each **dish** on the menu was served with chips and vegetables.
- A **stew** is usually meat and vegetables in a sauce cooked in a pot for quite a long time.
- The Italians eat a lot of **pasta**, such as spaghetti and ravioli.
- Many people eat **toast** for breakfast. It's bread which has been cooked on both sides and they often put butter and marmalade on it.

1 I think the restaurant is _____, so join the queue and choose what you want.
2 A _____ is a great meal to make for a cold winter's day, especially if you have plenty of time.
3 I'd love to try some of your curry, as long as it's not too _____.
4 I'm never very hungry in the morning and a cup of coffee and a slice of _____ is usually enough.
5 I don't like pizza, so when we go to an Italian restaurant I usually order _____.
6 Sarah's got a job as a _____ at the local hospital and she says it's really hard work.
7 People in some countries have a very poor _____ without enough vitamins.
8 Our chef is highly experienced and specialises in producing top quality European _____.
9 The food in other countries can seem a little strange at first but you soon _____ it.
10 The waiter came back and said that they'd run out of chicken pie so I had to order another _____.

Unit 7

EXAM PRACTICE — LISTENING PARTS 3 AND 4

Exam know-how

When you do Listening Part 3:
- Read the statements about each speaker first before you listen. Try to predict what language or ideas you might hear. When the cassette is played, listen out for your predictions. If you hear the keywords you expected, it may mean that is the right answer.

When you do Listening Part 4:
- Read the instructions and the questions or statements quickly before you listen. Try to anticipate what the people are going to be talking about. You might underline words in the questions or statements which you expect to hear. If you know what to expect, it will help you to understand what is being said.

A Part 3

You will hear five people talking about their experiences in different restaurants. For questions **1-5**, choose from the list **A-F** what happened to each speaker. Use the letters only once. There is one extra letter you do not need to use.

A I was expecting less choice.

Speaker 1 ☐ 1

B I was expecting a quieter place.

Speaker 2 ☐ 2

C I was expecting more polite waiters.

Speaker 3 ☐ 3

D I was expecting higher prices.

Speaker 4 ☐ 4

E I was expecting a busier place.

Speaker 5 ☐ 5

F I was expecting better service.

B Part 4

You will hear an interview with a chef about a cookery programme on TV. For questions **6-12**, decide which of the statements are TRUE and which are FALSE. Write **T** for True or **F** for False in the boxes provided.

6	Trisha was offered this series because of a previous success.	6
7	Patrick was tested before being offered a part on the show.	7
8	*Leave it to Cook* is meant to make difficult techniques easier.	8
9	Patrick thinks he is a good example for the viewers.	9
10	Patrick thinks people should make a great effort to eat well.	10
11	Patrick's children love the things he makes for them.	11
12	Trisha suggests listeners should be imaginative in their cooking.	12

Grammar focus

First, complete the following table using the words in the box.

| absolutely   wonderful   very   expensive |

	examples	we can use these expressions
gradable adjectives	big, cheap, interesting, _____, etc	a little, too, quite, extremely, _____
ungradable adjectives	perfect, amazing, exhausted, _____, etc	totally, completely, quite, _____

Now look at the following sentences using the word 'quite' in two different ways.

*I thought the food was **quite** spicy.*
*I thought the food was **quite** excellent.*

In the first sentence, 'quite' means 'fairly'. That's because 'spicy' is a gradable adjective, and the sentence is the same as:

*I thought the food was **fairly** spicy.*

In the second sentence, 'quite' means 'absolutely, completely'. That's because 'excellent' is an ungradable adjective, and the sentence is the same as:

*I thought the food was **absolutely** excellent.*

Listen to these statements. For each one, decide whether the word 'quite' means 'fairly' or 'absolutely' by circling the correct answer.

Statement 1	Statement 2	Statement 3	Statement 4	Statement 5
a fairly	a fairly	a fairly	a fairly	a fairly
b absolutely	b absolutely	b absolutely	b absolutely	b absolutely

Listening and Speaking Skills / Unit 7

Unit 8

The Media

WARM-UP — Pairwork

Look at the pictures. In pairs, decide to what extent you agree or disagree with the following statements and explain why.
- It would be exciting to be a reporter in a war zone.
- The media should be careful to present a balanced view.
- When a few powerful people control the media, we get a better service.

DEVELOP YOUR SPEAKING SKILLS

A Dos and Don'ts

Which of these are good things for you to say or do in the interview?
Which of them are not so good? Write **Do** or **Don't** before each one.

1 _____ interrupt your partner in Part 2 to say you agree or disagree.
2 _____ give your opinion briefly after your partner's turn in Part 2.
3 _____ say things like 'You're wrong!' or 'That's rubbish!'.
4 _____ agree and disagree in a polite, friendly way in Part 3.
5 _____ continue to agree and disagree with your partner in Part 4.
6 _____ try to use phrases apart from 'I agree' or 'I disagree'.
7 _____ explain why you agree or disagree with your partner.
8 _____ ask your partner whether they agree with you or not.
9 _____ use the expression 'What do you think?' all the time.
10 _____ ask your partner different questions about their opinion.

B Listen and circle

Listen to the following extracts taken from different interviews with students. For each student, choose the phrase you hear them use to agree or disagree.

Student 1
a In a way, you have right ...
b In a way, you are right ...

Student 2
a I would agree with ...
b I could agree with ...

Student 3
a I'm not agree with you ...
b I don't agree with you ...

Student 4
a I partly agree with you ...
b I am partly agree with you ...

Student 5
a I agree with you to a certain extent ...
b I agree with you up to a certain extent ...

Student 6
a As Mary had said, ...
b As Mary said, ...

C What are they used for?

Apart from the phrases the students used in B, the following words or phrases can also be used to agree or disagree. Put them in the correct box.

b You've got a point, but ...	a Absolutely.	c But what about ...
c Surely, though, ...	a I totally agree ...	b I agree in part ...
a Yes, I hadn't thought of that.	b To some extent, that's right ...	a You're right, and ...
c I have to disagree ...	c I'm afraid I don't agree ...	a That's absolutely right, ...
a That's quite true, and ...	a I couldn't agree more ...	a That's a very good point ...
a Exactly.	b I agree with you up to a point ...	
a That's what I was thinking.	b There's a lot in what you say, but ...	

Phrases we can use to ...

agree a	partly agree or disagree b	disagree c
I completely agree.	*I partly agree.*	*I completely disagree.*

Listening and Speaking Skills / Unit 8

Unit 8

DEVELOP YOUR SPEAKING SKILLS

D Discuss *Pairwork*

In pairs, take it in turns to read the following statements to each other and to agree or disagree. Try to use as many of the phrases from B and C as you can. Remember to give reasons for your opinions.

The internet is going to become a bigger and bigger part of our lives.

What newspapers say should be controlled by the government. We should make sure that nobody writes anything bad about the people in power.

TV programmes for children should all be educational and whether kids enjoy them or not is not really very important.

TV news programmes are better at informing the public than newspapers are.

E Classroom debate

Your teacher will divide you into two groups, Group A and Group B. You are going to discuss the statement:

'This class believes that using the internet in English lessons would be a good thing.'

Group A: You are 'for' the statement. Below are three points that Group B is going to make against the statement. On the right, make notes about why you disagree with these points.

Group B's 'against' points	Why we disagree
1 It would waste a lot of time.	1 _____
2 It wouldn't help with our English.	2 _____
3 It would be too expensive.	3 _____

Group B: You are 'against' the statement. Below are three points that Group A is going to make for the statement. Underneath, make notes about why you disagree with these points.

Group A's 'for' points
1 It would be fun and motivating.
2 We could contact people by e-mail.
3 It would teach us about computers.

Why we disagree
1 _____
2 _____
3 _____

F Debate the point

Now hold your debate. Your teacher will guide you and tell you what to do. When you have used all the points from the boxes above, continue with other ideas. Remember to use good phrases to agree and disagree.

Wordperfect

Read these sentences and then use the words in bold to complete the sentences below.

- The **editor** sent his two best reporters out to get the story.
- According to the **TV listings/guide**, there's a film on Channel Five at ten o'clock.
- I don't believe in **censorship**. I think that people should be free to write whatever they want.
- Some people pay for **satellite TV** and they have a kind of dish on their roof to receive the signal from space.
- Have you seen the new **commercial/ad/ advert/advertisement** for soap powder with the funny dog?
- The **presenter** of the show introduced her first guest, who was a famous actor.
- A **celebrity** is a person who is famous, such as a singer or actor.
- A **sponsor** is a company that pays for a TV show, a sporting event, and so on.
- The **newsreader** said that there had been a plane crash in Russia.
- Stay with us, and after the **break** we'll be bringing you more pictures of that skateboarding dog!

1 I know you say that she's supposed to be a _____, but I've never heard of her!

2 You have to have a good voice and look serious to be a _____; most of them are also trained journalists.

3 We're thinking of getting _____, but I think the dish looks so ugly on top of the house.

4 If you feel that strongly about it, why don't you write a letter to the _____?

5 Wasn't that actress in a _____ for a bank a couple of years ago?

6 The government have been accused of _____ after they tried to stop the newspapers printing the truth.

7 The channel lost its _____ after making a programme that criticised the fast food industry.

8 She used to be a _____ on a children's TV programme, and now she hosts a game show.

9 We're going to take a quick _____, but stay tuned for more.

10 Could you pass me the _____ then I can see what time it starts?

Listening and Speaking Skills / Unit 8   49

Unit 8

EXAM PRACTICE — SPEAKING PARTS 3 AND 4

Exam know-how

When you do Speaking Part 3:
- Try to use as many different ways of agreeing and disagreeing as you can. Ask your partner for his or her opinion in different ways, too. Try not to use 'What do you think?' and 'I agree' too much.

When you do Speaking Part 4:
- Remember that this is supposed to be a discussion between you, your partner and the examiner. It's okay to say, 'I agree with Mary ...', but it's even better to turn to your partner and say, 'I agree with you ...'. This shows the examiner that you are a good communicator.

A Part 3

> I'd like you to imagine that you work for a TV news programme. These pictures show the events that have happened today. I'd like you to discuss how important you think each event is and then decide together which three events you would like to include in tonight's programme. Remember, you have about three minutes for this.

3 MIN

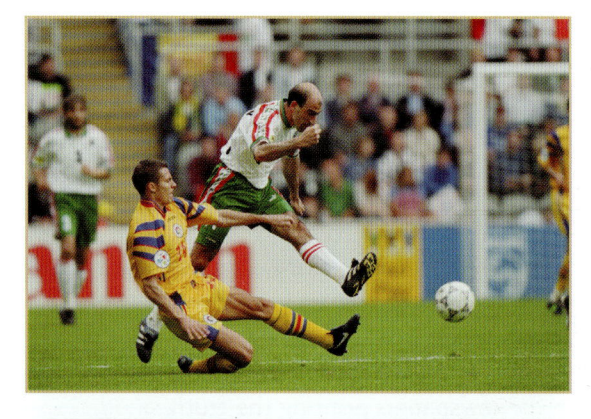

B Part 4 4 min

- Do you think there's too much news on TV?
- Do you think having more channels would be a good thing?
- Is TV entertainment or is it education?
- Do you think watching TV can help to improve your English?
- How could TV be improved in your country?
- Do you think the internet can help students?
- How often do you use the internet?

Grammar focus

Look at the following sentences using the verb 'agree' and notice which prepositions are used.

We couldn't **agree on** a video to watch for the evening.
Mum **agreed to** our suggestion about which film to watch.
We never seem to **agree about** television programmes.
I have to say that I don't **agree with** Bill.
I really don't **agree with** allowing children to use the internet.

Circle the correct words to complete the rules.

We use (with) / on when we are talking about a person. + name.
We use (about) / to when we are talking about a subject for discussion. + noun
We use to / (with) when we are talking about morally approving of something. + ing.
We use (on) / with when we are talking about reaching a decision.
We use on / (to) when we are talking about giving permission or accepting a suggestion.

Complete the following sentences by writing the correct prepositions in the spaces provided.

1. We have to agree ___on___ two things to include in our TV programme. (decision)
2. I agree ___with___ you in part, but I think you're forgetting an important point.
3. Hopefully, the headmaster will agree ~~to with~~ our suggestion that we connect the school to the internet.
4. I don't agree ___with___ having violent films on in the early evening.
5. You and I will never agree ___on___ the role of TV in today's world.

Listening and Speaking / Unit 8   51

Unit 9

The Weather

WARM-UP Pairwork

Look at the pictures. In pairs, ask and answer the following questions:
- How do you prefer to find out about the weather?
- Are you interested in knowing what the forecast is every day?
- Why is the weather forecast so important to some people?
- How accurate do you think weather forecasts are?

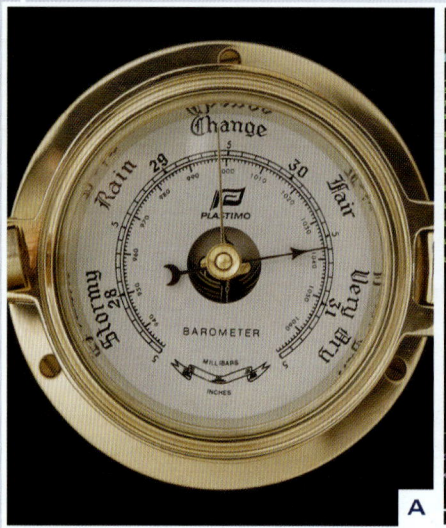

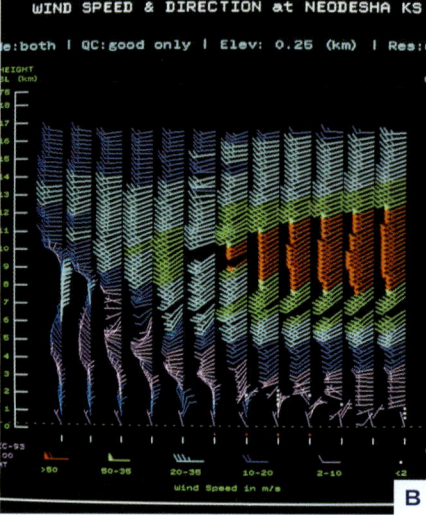

A   B   C

DEVELOP YOUR LISTENING SKILLS

A True or false?
Look at these statements about Listening Part 2.
Decide if they are true or false. Circle **T** for True and **F** for False.

1 Listening Part 2 is always a gap-filling/note-taking exercise.   T / F
2 You can only write one word in each gap.   T / F
3 You might have to write as many as ten words in one gap.   T / F
4 The exact word or phrase that you need to write is always in the listening somewhere.   T / F
5 The gaps are in the same order as the information which you hear.   T / F
6 Your answer is always marked wrong if you make a spelling mistake.   T / F
7 You can write numbers in a gap, where appropriate.   T / F

B What goes in a gap?

In Listening Part 2, you have to fill ten gaps by writing a word or short phrase in each gap. Look at these three examples of gaps.

1 Temperature tomorrow: [_____] **1**

2 What will the temperature be tomorrow? [_____] **2**

3 The temperature tomorrow will be [_____] **3**

Now think about possible kinds of answers.

Example:
Write an answer involving a number which fits in all three gaps: __25__

Now write down one word which would fit all three gaps: _____

Finally, write a phrase (of between two and five words) which fits all three gaps:
_____

C Discuss (Pairwork)

As a class, discuss your choices.
How many different words or phrases fit all three gaps?

Here is another gap.
Do your choices fit this gap too? If not, discuss why not.

4 The temperature tomorrow will be [_____] **4** today.

D Which fit?

Look at these words and phrases.
Decide which of the gaps above they can fill, if any. Tick or cross.

		gap 1	gap 2	gap 3	gap 4
1	42				
2	42°	✓	✓	✓	✗
3	forty-two degrees	✓	✓	✓	
4	cool	✓	✓	✓	✗
5	cooler than	✗	✗	✗	✓
6	coolest	✗	✗	✗	✗
7	cooler than yesterday	✓	✓	✓	✗
8	coolness	✗	✗	✗	✗

Listening and Speaking Skills / Unit 9

Unit 9

DEVELOP YOUR LISTENING SKILLS

E **Listen and write 1**

You are going to listen to the beginning of a weather forecast. As you listen, write one word in each gap to complete the sentences.

1. The temperature tomorrow will be [hotter] **1** than today.

2. There is not much [humidity] **2** in the air.

3. Tomorrow will be [bright] **3** , especially at noon.

4. There will not be much [cloud.] **4**

F **Listen and write 2**

Now listen again. This time, all your answers will be phrases of between two and five words, or will involve numbers.

Today:

highest temperature: [38°] **1**

Tomorrow:

up to 44 degrees in: [parts of the S.E.] **2**

humidity (per cent): [16%] **3**

bright, particularly around midday and [in the early afternoon] **4**

54

Wordperfect

G Make a guess

Here are some more gaps for the same weather forecast. Can you remember any of the answers? Write a word or short phrase in each one. It doesn't matter if it is only a guess.

1 What is the name of the weather presenter?
| Elaine | 1 |

2 What is the country experiencing at the moment?
| heatwave | 2 |

3 Where will it be hottest tomorrow?
| parts of SE | 3 |

4 The air will not contain much
| humidity | 4 |
tomorrow.

5 People will not be
| sweating | 5 |
much tomorrow.

6 There won't be much
| cloud. | 6 |
for most of the day.

7 What should people wear outside?
| Sunscreen. | 7 |

H Listen and check

Now listen one more time and check your answers to G. Change any of the guesses that you got wrong.

Read these sentences and then use the words in bold to complete the sentences below.

- We were **snowed in** for three days and couldn't even get to the shops.
- If the river rises any higher, the whole town is in danger of **flooding**.
- If it carries on raining, then the river may well burst its **banks**.
- The weatherman said that we're in for a cold **spell** over the next few days.
- These days, **meteorologists** rely on sophisticated computers to forecast the weather.
- It was so **windy** that my umbrella kept turning inside out!
- Let's go for a walk in the country if it's **sunny** tomorrow.
- You'd better take your **waterproofs**. They say it's going to rain quite heavily later.
- **Hail** is small pieces of ice which fall from the sky.
- If it is **drizzling**, it's raining very lightly.

1 I got caught in a _____ storm. It was actually quite painful!
2 It's only _____. I'm not going to bother to take my umbrella.
3 We had a really hot _____ last week. It was lovely. We had a barbecue in the garden every evening.
4 I hope we don't get _____. I've got an important meeting tomorrow.
5 Remember to bring your _____. They'll keep you warm and dry if the weather turns bad.
6 The regular _____ could be avoided if the council put in a proper drainage system. At the moment, there's nowhere for the water to flow to.
7 Do you think it's too _____ to fly my kite?
8 The local council are strengthening the _____ of the river in an attempt to prevent a repeat of last year's flooding.
9 Are all the weathermen and weathergirls on TV professional _____?
10 It was a beautiful _____ day. There wasn't a cloud in the sky.

Unit 9

EXAM PRACTICE — LISTENING PARTS 1 AND 2

Exam know-how

When you do Listening Part 2:
- Remember that you might have to write a short phrase. If you write more than five words, your answer is probably too long. Don't write too much information.
- The gaps are always in the same order as the information on the cassette. For example, if you haven't heard the answer to question 4 and then you hear the answer to question 5, you'll know the answer to question 4 comes before that.

A Part 1

You will hear people talking in eight different situations. For questions **1-8**, choose the best answer, **A**, **B** or **C**.

1. You hear a man talking about a football match. Why was the match cancelled?
   A because of the bad weather — *pouring w rain*
   B because of football hooligans
   C because of an accident — *bus crashed — weren't going to make it*   [C] 1

2. You hear someone talking on a mobile phone. Who is she talking to?
   A a customer — *talking about*
   (B) a colleague — *desk file*
   C a relative — *John's house — staying with*   [B] 2

3. You overhear two people in a travel agent's arguing about a trip. What do they disagree about?
   A how warm it will be — *You need to take a jumper. chilly. Colder*
   B how sunny it will be
   C how humid it will be — *you mean if it's too humid — agree.*   [A] 3

4. You hear a weather forecast on the radio. What will the weather be like tomorrow in the North?
   A wet
   (B) windy — *gales — hold on to hats.*
   C bright   [B] 4

5. Listen to this news report about a flood. What was the probable cause of the flood? — *it's now a river*
   A a river bursting its banks
   B a broken pipe — *burst pipe why this happened.*
   C heavy rainfall — *no rain.*   [B] 5

6. You hear two academics talking on television about global warming. What are they arguing about?
   A the existence of global warming — *all agree.*
   B the causes of global warming — *open to debate. responsible — human race*
   C the effects of global warming   [B] 6

7. Listen to this man talking about the weather. Who is he?
   A a vet
   (B) a farmer — *600 beef cattle healthy & well-fed.*
   C a butcher — *meat (d)*   [B] 7

8. Listen to this woman talking about weather forecasting. How does she feel?
   (A) angry
   B worried — *they failed to predict it can't get it right it's laughable*
   C amused   [A] 8

56

B Part 2

You will hear a radio presenter talking about an internet website. For questions **9-18**, fill in the missing information with a word or short phrase.

Search & Find Factsheet No. 22

name of website:	[_____ 9 _____]
website address:	www.ww.co.uk
subject:	strange weather in [_____ 10 _____]
such as:	raining frogs, stones, [_____ 11 _____], lizards
site also includes:	✓ other useful [_____ 12 _____]
	✓ [_____ 13 _____] page
	(with more than [_____ 14 _____])
	✓ [_____ 15 _____] of meteorological terms
	(with photos or [_____ 16 _____])
	✓ links to other websites
ideal for:	[_____ 17 _____] working on projects
website designed by:	students at [_____ 18 _____]

Grammar focus

When people speak, they often run certain words and phrases together. Listen to this example.
Does it sound like this?

*Are you **going to** make a decision now, or **do you want to wait and see** what the **weather is** like?*

Or this?

*Are you **gonna** make a decision now, or **d'ya wanna wait'n'see** what the **weather's** like?*

Listen to these people talking. For each one, fill in the gaps with the written form of the word or phrase they say (i.e. write 'going to' and not 'gonna').

1 You _____ out in such bad weather. What _____ thinking?
2 I think _____ in the morning, whatever _____ like.
3 _____ use a flash, as the sun's quite bright anyway.
4 I _____. I _____ weather forecast this morning.
5 They _____ come if it's snowing. The _____ bad, and _____ be _____ them to do on the farm. _____ a ring in the morning _____ if _____.

Listening and Speaking Skills / Unit 9

Unit 10 The Environment

WARM-UP Pairwork

Look at the pictures. Match them with the types of housing below.
Now, in pairs, discuss which of these you would prefer to live in. Give reasons for your choice.

flat _____   detached house _____   terraced house _____   bungalow _____   semi-detached house _____

DEVELOP YOUR SPEAKING SKILLS

A Dos and Don'ts

Which of these are good things for a candidate to say or do in Speaking Part 2?
Which of them are not so good? Write **Do** or **Don't** before each one.

If you are not sure exactly what the picture is, ...

1 _____ panic.
2 _____ stop talking.
3 _____ say that you are not sure.
4 _____ say that you can't do the task.
5 _____ use words and phrases that express doubt and possibility.
6 _____ give reasons when you express your opinion.

B Listen and tick or cross

You're going to hear two students talking about a photograph in Part 2. They are unsure exactly what the photo is, and they express their uncertainty. Which of these words and phrases do they use? Listen and tick the ones you hear.

Student 1
1. It must be ... _____
2. It may be ... _____
3. I think ... _____
4. I believe ... _____
5. probably _____
6. definitely _____
7. maybe _____
8. I hope that ... _____
9. I don't really understand ... _____

Student 2
1. maybe _____
2. I may be ... _____
3. It might be ... _____
4. I know ... _____
5. I think ... _____
6. I can't tell you if ... _____
7. I can't really understand if ... _____

C Listen and write

Now listen again. Each student uses one other good phrase for expressing uncertainty. Write their phrases on the lines provided.

Student 1 _____
Student 2 _____

D What are they used for?

Here are some more words and phrases you could use in Speaking Part 2. Write each one in its correct box. The words and phrases already in the boxes are from the previous exercises.

It can't be ...	Judging from ...	I'm not really/totally sure, but ...
I would imagine that ...	It's not clear ...	It has to be ...
It could be ...	It's difficult to tell, but ...	It's quite likely that ...
I guess that ...		

Expressing uncertainty
I can't really make out ...
_____
_____
_____

Expressing possibility
It may be ...
It might be ...
probably
maybe
I think ...
I suppose that ...
_____
_____
_____
_____

Expressing certainty
It must be
definitely
_____
_____
_____

Listening and Speaking Skills / Unit 10

Unit 10

DEVELOP YOUR SPEAKING SKILLS

E Look and make notes
Look at these two photographs, and make notes on the lines provided to answer the questions.

Picture A
1 What is this a picture of?
   _____
2 What are the two or three most important things in the picture?
   _____
3 Can we tell if it's a town or a city? _____
4 Which do you think it is? Why?
   _____
5 Do you think it's a town/city in your country? _____
6 Why/Why not? _____
7 Do you like this place? _____
8 Why/Why not? _____

Picture B
1 What is this a picture of?
   _____
2 What are the two or three most important things in this photo?
   _____
3 Where do you think the photo was taken? _____
4 Why? _____
5 Do you like this place? _____
6 Why/Why not? _____

Both pictures

1 What is the main difference between the pictures?
_____

2 Which place would you prefer to visit?
_____

3 Why? _____

F *Compare and contrast*

In pairs, look at the photographs again and practise comparing and contrasting using the useful phrases in D, and your notes in E. One of you should read the examiner's words and then listen. When you have finished, swap roles.

Here are two pictures of different places. I'd like you to compare and contrast these pictures, saying which place you would prefer to visit, and why. Remember you only have one minute for this.

1 min

Wordperfect

Read these sentences and then use the words in bold to complete the sentences below.

- It's very peaceful in the **country(side)**, but there aren't as many facilities as in the town.
- We went to a **safari park** last week. It's much better than a zoo as the animals have plenty of room to roam around.
- The government has decided to **ban** fox hunting. They believe it's cruel and unnecessary.
- We should think of the Earth as a large **ecosystem**. All the animals and plants depend on each other.
- If the **rainforests** are all destroyed, millions of different types of insect will become extinct.
- Are cars that take **diesel** more environmentally-friendly than cars that take petrol?
- This newspaper is printed on **recycled** paper.
- Too many factories dispose of their **waste** by pumping it into rivers and the sea.
- **CFCs** are the chemicals responsible for much of the damage to the ozone layer.
- Individuals can't solve the world's environmental problems on their own; governments and **industry** must change too.

1 Make sure your deodorant doesn't contain harmful _____; you don't want to increase the size of the hole of the ozone layer!

2 Could you fill the tank up with _____, please?

3 They're going to _____ cars from the city centre in an attempt to reduce pollution from exhaust fumes.

4 We should all try to reduce household _____ by taking all our glass, paper and plastic to recycling bins.

5 Once you enter the _____, do not get out of your cars. The animals are dangerous.

6 The whole _____ of the region was changed when the airport was built. Most of the wild birds have completely disappeared.

7 We've decided to move to the _____ as it's a much safer place to bring up small children.

8 The _____ are so far away that it's difficult for us in the West to see the damage.

9 Many people who work in _____ are trying hard to make their companies more environmentally aware and responsible.

10 This _____ glass is just as good as brand-new glass.

Unit 10

EXAM PRACTICE — SPEAKING PARTS 1 AND 2

Exam know-how

When you do Speaking Part 2:
- Try not to say 'I can see ...' when you are talking about the photos. It sounds much more natural if you say 'There's ...' or 'There are ...'.
- Remember that you will not lose marks if you say you're not sure about something. On the contrary, you will impress the examiner with your ability to express your uncertainty.

A Part 1   3 MIN

We'd like to know something about you, so I'm going to ask you some questions about yourselves.

- How long have you lived there?
- What are the worst things about living there?
- Is there anything you would change about where you live?
- What would you change about your home?
- What are the best things about living there?
- Would you prefer to live somewhere else? Why/Why not?
- What kind of building do you live in?
- Do you live in the town or the countryside?
- How environmentally-friendly are you?

B Part 2   1 MIN

Photos for Candidate A:

Candidate A, I'd like you to compare and contrast these pictures, saying how you think the people in the pictures feel.

Candidate B, how would you feel if you were in these situations?   20 SECS

Photos for Candidate B:

Candidate B, I'd like you to compare and contrast these pictures, saying what you think happens in these places.

1 min

Candidate A, which place would you prefer to work in?

20 SECS

Grammar *focus*

Read the following sentences and choose the correct paraphrase in each case.

1 You **must** find it noisy living in a city.
a I think you probably find living in a city noisy. (*deduction*)
b I really want you to find it noisy living in a city. (*obligation*)

2 You **must** make more of an effort to recycle.
a I think you probably make more of an effort to recycle. (*deduction*)
b I really want you to make more of an effort to recycle. (*obligation*)

Rewrite the following sentences using the words in bold and the word 'must'.
Write between two and five words. Do not change the word given.

1 Because there is a lot of pollution, I think the man in the photo feels depressed.
   feel
   The man in the photo _____ there is so much pollution.
2 The local council is responsible for making sure that the beaches are clean.
   make
   The local council _____ that the beaches are clean.
3 Judging by all the pollution, I think this is a photo of an industrial area.
   of
   This photo _____ an industrial area, judging by all the pollution.
4 The photographer probably took this photograph in a wood or forest.
   have
   This photograph _____ in a wood or forest.

Listening and Speaking Skills / Unit 10 63

Unit 11 Technology

WARM-UP *Pairwork*

Look at the pictures. In pairs, discuss the following questions:
- Do you own any of the things in the photos?
- Approximately how much do they usually cost?
- What functions do these things usually have?
- Which ones would you like to have? Why?

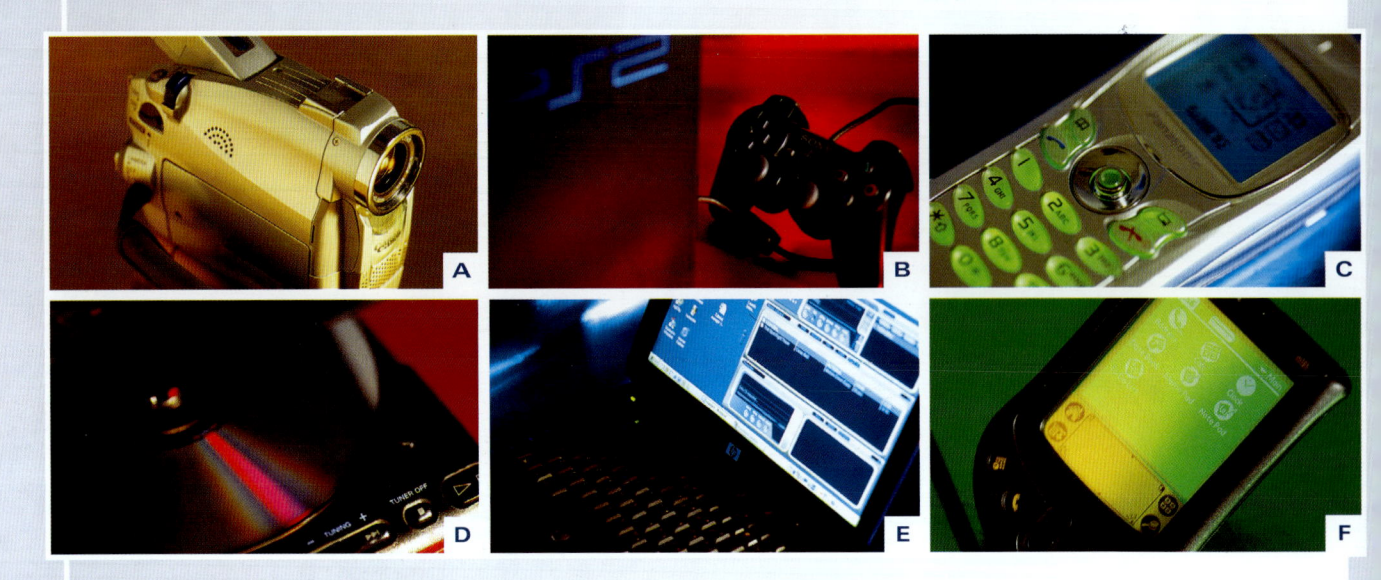

A   B   C
D   E   F

DEVELOP YOUR LISTENING SKILLS

A Who are they?

You are going to listen to five teenagers. They are each taking part in a local radio show called 'Buy and Sell.' In the show, people phone up and leave a message describing something that they want to buy second-hand or something that they want to sell. First, listen to their names, ages and phone numbers and write the information on the lines provided.

Name	Age	Phone number
1		
2		
3		
4		
5		

B Are they buying or selling?

Now listen to what they say next. Do they want to buy or sell something? Tick the correct column.

Buy	Sell
1 _____	_____
2 _____	_____
3 _____	_____
4 _____	_____
5 _____	_____

C What's it like?

Now listen to their complete messages. Circle the correct words or phrases to complete the notepad.

Buy and Sell

1. Ticon X3-400 / X34-100 camera
   black / blue
   case included / extra
   £25 / £20

2. CD / DVD player
   must be easy to carry / use
   with headphones / earphones
   not more than £50 / £15

3. video recorder / camera
   must / mustn't have rechargeable batteries
   around £14 / £40

4. mountain / racing bike
   in very / fairly good condition
   make: Taylor's / Tiler's
   8 / 18 gears
   price: £65 / £56

5. electric / electronic organiser
   model: Handmate / Handmade Vdx
   price: £120 / £80

Unit 11

DEVELOP YOUR LISTENING SKILLS

D Listen and write

Listen one more time. For each question, write a word or short phrase on the line provided.

Message 1
What kind of photographs does he say the camera takes? _____
Will he consider lowering the price? _____

Message 2
Why won't she consider paying more? _____

Message 3
What does she not mind about? _____
Who advised her to get one with rechargeable batteries? _____

Message 4
What kind of phone does he have? _____
What reason does he give for selling his bike? _____
How old is the bike? _____
What depends on distance? _____

Message 5
When was her birthday? _____
When did she get the organiser? _____
How much will someone save by buying this organiser? _____

E Fill in the card!

Imagine you want to buy or sell something on 'Buy and Sell'. First fill in this information card. Don't show anyone else your information.

```
Name:                   _____
Age:                    _____
Phone number:           _____
Buy or sell?            _____
Item:                   _____
Make/model number:      _____
Age of product:         _____
Condition:              _____
Description:            _____
Any other information:  _____
```

Wordperfect

F 'Buy and Sell'!

As a class, take turns to say your messages. Imagine you are leaving the message on an answerphone so it can be played on the radio. When someone else is saying their message, note down their information on one of the cards below.

```
Name:                  _____
Age:                   _____
Phone number:          _____
Buy or sell?           _____
Item:                  _____
Make/model
number:                _____
Age of product:        _____
Condition:             _____
Description:           _____
Any other
information:           _____
```

```
Name:                  _____
Age:                   _____
Phone number:          _____
Buy or sell?           _____
Item:                  _____
Make/model
number:                _____
Age of product:        _____
Condition:             _____
Description:           _____
Any other
information:           _____
```

Read these sentences and then use the words in bold to complete the sentences below.

- I love **surfing the (inter)net**. There are so many interesting websites these days.
- I used to find it hard to keep in touch with old friends but with **e-mail/email**, it's so easy.
- We spent the whole Physics lesson doing experiments in the science **lab(oratory)** at school. It was great fun.
- The word '**drugs**' can be used to refer to both narcotics and pharmaceuticals.
- I can't open that file you sent me by e-mail. Our word processors are just not **compatible**.
- Robbie quickly picked up the telephone **receiver** and said, 'Hello?'
- I'll send you a **text message** to let you know I arrived. You'll have your mobile on, won't you?
- I'm thinking of getting a **wide-screen TV**. I hear they're much better for watching films on.
- I use **teletext** all the time. It's very useful for finding out travel and weather information. You just turn on the TV!
- Most laptop computers and mobile phones have got a **rechargeable battery** inside.

1 I got a _____ from Emma which said: how r u? wanna meet @ 8pm tonite & c a film? :-)

2 British plugs are not _____ with European sockets, so you need an adaptor if you take electrical equipment abroad.

3 My new phone's got a speakerphone, so you don't need to hold the _____.

4 I never write letters but I must write to about ten people a day by _____.

5 I must get a new _____ for my video camera. It runs down so quickly these days.

6 Did you know that caffeine, alcohol and aspirin are all _____?

7 Please be careful in the _____. There are a lot of dangerous chemicals in there.

8 _____ is very addictive. It's easy to spend hours in front of your computer.

9 In a few years' time, you'll have to have a _____. You won't be able to watch any programmes on the one you've got now.

10 Not all TVs can receive _____. You have to get one with a special button on the remote control.

Listening and Speaking Skills / Unit 11

Unit 11

EXAM PRACTICE — LISTENING PARTS 3 AND 4

Exam know-how

When you do the Listening Paper:
- There may well be some words you hear that you don't know. Don't panic! Try to work out what they must mean from the words around them that you do know. Sometimes, they won't be important anyway because you often only have to understand the general meaning to answer the question.

When you do Listening Part 4:
- This part is sometimes multiple choice. If you are unsure of the answer to a question, ask yourself which option is definitely wrong. If you are still unsure which of the two remaining options is the answer, make a guess. Don't leave any answers blank when you fill in your Answer Sheet.

A Part 3

You will hear five people talking about different technological items. For questions 1-5, choose from the list of items **A-F** what each speaker is describing. Use the letters only once. There is one extra letter you do not need to use.

A a digital camera

Speaker 1 [ ] 1

B a video camera

Speaker 2 [ ] 2

C a video recorder

Speaker 3 [ ] 3

D a mobile phone

Speaker 4 [ ] 4

E a remote control

Speaker 5 [ ] 5

F an electronic organiser

B Part 4

You will hear a radio interview about a popular website. For questions **6-12**, decide which of the choices, **A**, **B** or **C**, is the correct answer.

6 When did the website go online?
   A two and a half years ago
   B a year and a half ago
   C exactly a year ago

7 How many people have visited the website so far?
   A approximately 250,000
   B almost a million
   C more than 8,000,000

8 The website's popularity is due partly to the fact that
   A people have very close friends these days.
   B it's not easy to stay in contact with people from your past.
   C more and more people want to organise reunions.

9 Marjorie believes that we want to know
   A if the people we knew are more successful than us.
   B what the people we knew are doing in their lives.
   C if the people we knew remember us.

10 Where was the story about the couple publicised?
    A on the website
    B in the newspapers
    C in a department store

11 What does Marjorie say about their plans for the future?
    A They want to spend even more time running the website.
    B They want to take a short holiday in the near future.
    C They want to spend some of the money they've earned.

12 Steve says that they are planning to
    A start another website similar to the one they now run.
    B need to have more people working on their next website.
    C continue to create original websites in the future.

Grammar focus

Look at these three words: can   go   make

At first sight, they look like verbs, but they can also be used as nouns:

I bought a **can** of lemonade.
It's my **go**!
What **make** of car does your father drive?

Listen to these sentences. Decide whether the word is being used as a verb or a noun.

1 e-mail   verb / noun
2 water   verb / noun
3 phone   verb / noun
4 watch   verb / noun
5 read   verb / noun
6 drug   verb / noun

Listening and Speaking Skills / Unit 11

Unit 12 Health and Fitness

WARM-UP (Pairwork)

Look at the pictures. Can you match them to the words below?
Now, in pairs, discuss what the following things are used for.
Have you ever had to use any of these things yourself?

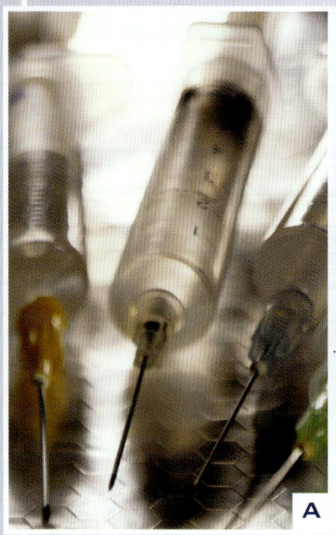

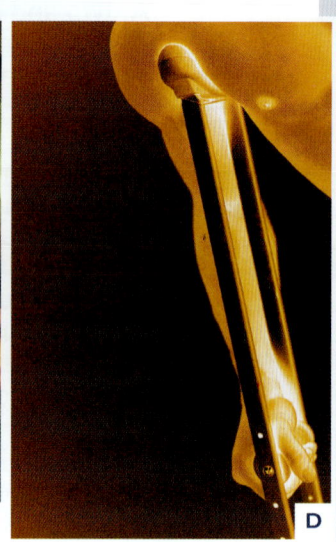

crutches ____   a sling ____   plaster ____   a syringe ____

DEVELOP YOUR SPEAKING SKILLS

A Dos and Don'ts

Which of these are good things for a candidate to say or do in the Speaking paper? Which of them are not so good?
Write **Do** or **Don't** before each one.

1. _____ make all your answers and responses as short as possible.
2. _____ make all your sentences as short as possible.
3. _____ keep your grammar as simple as possible.
4. _____ correct yourself if you realise you've made a grammatical mistake.
5. _____ think: 'If I try to use more complex grammar, and make a mistake, I'll lose marks.'
6. _____ use connectors like 'but', 'and', 'if', 'because'.
7. _____ use relative pronouns like 'that', 'which', 'who', 'where', 'when'.
8. _____ use linking devices like 'First of all', 'Having said that', 'And so'.
9. _____ worry that the examiner may disagree with your opinions.
10. _____ think: 'It doesn't matter if what I say is illogical, as long as my English is good.'
11. _____ use very formal English.

B Listen and tick

You are going to hear an extract from two candidates doing Part 3 of the Speaking Paper. Tick the words or phrases you hear them say.

		1st candidate	2nd candidate
1	Well,		
2	but		
3	also		
4	or		
5	because		
6	the first one		
7	and		
8	if		
9	it's		

C Discuss

Pairwork

In pairs, discuss how well you think the candidates did. Did they use fairly long and complex sentences? Were they logical? Did they give reasons for their opinions? Did they make any mistakes? If they did, do you think they will lose marks because of them? Listen again to the cassette, if necessary.

D The one-minute game

In pairs, look at these different jobs.

> G.P.   surgeon   chemist   nurse
> ambulance driver   dentist   vet

Student A:
- Talk for one minute about one of the jobs.
- You can talk about what that person does, or if you would like to have that job, but you must not stop talking, and you mustn't say anything illogical.
- Try to use connecting words and phrases to make your sentences longer.
- Don't worry at all about making grammatical mistakes.

Student B:
- You are responsible for the timing, and for listening to your partner.
- You must say 'Stop!' if your partner pauses for more than two seconds, or if your partner says anything illogical. If they don't, stop your partner after one minute.
- Don't stop your partner if they make a grammatical mistake.

When you have finished, swap roles and choose another job.

Listening and Speaking Skills / Unit 12

Unit 12

DEVELOP YOUR LISTENING SKILLS

E Listen and circle

You are going to hear three students answering questions in Part 4. For each student, circle **T** for True and **F** for False. You may need to listen to the cassette twice.

Student 1
1 The question was 'How important is it to have a healthy diet?' **T / F**
2 The student gives two reasons why something is good for your health. **T / F**
3 The student only gives one reason why something is good for your appearance. **T / F**

Student 2
1 The question was 'What are the best ways to stay fit and healthy?' **T / F**
2 The student gives two examples. **T / F**
3 The student makes only one suggestion. **T / F**

Student 3
1 The question was 'How important is it to keep fit?' **T / F**
2 The student gives two reasons why something is good for your health. **T / F**
3 The student mentions the result of exercising. **T / F**

F Match to make sense

The words and phrases in bold are all used to introduce a contrasting point of view. Match the two halves of each comment so that they make logical sense.

1 Private doctors often treat you more politely. _____
2 It's very sensible to exercise regularly. _____
3 I do try to have a healthy, balanced diet. _____
4 Turning a room at home into a gym is a possible solution. _____
5 My sister Carly's a vegetarian. _____

a **Having said that**, she does eat chicken occasionally.
b **On the other hand**, the equipment can be very expensive.
c **Mind you**, people who become obsessed with working out really annoy me.
d **But** they're very expensive, of course.
e **Though** there's nothing like a burger and chips every now and then.

Wordperfect

G Make notes

Here are three Part 4 questions. Think about your answers and make notes on the lines provided.

1 *How important is it to keep fit?*
   Two reasons why it's important:
   _____
   _____
   Example(s):
   _____
   _____
   Contrasting point:
   _____

2 *How important is it to have a healthy diet?*
   Two reasons why it's important:
   _____
   _____
   Example(s):
   _____
   _____
   Contrasting point:
   _____

3 *What are the best ways to stay fit and healthy?*
   Two or three best ways:
   _____
   _____
   _____
   Reason(s):
   _____
   _____
   Contrasting point:
   _____

H Ask and answer

In pairs, ask and answer the three questions in G.

Read these sentences and then use the words in bold to complete the sentences below.

- When I broke my leg playing rugby, I was **in plaster** for six weeks.
- Mum, I've cut my finger! Have you got a **plaster**?
- A **consultant** is a doctor who specialises in a certain area of medicine.
- She's sprained her wrist, so her arm's in a **sling** at the moment.
- The health system in Britain is called the National Health Service, or the **NHS**.
- I've got to take these **antibiotics** three times a day for a week.
- Dan is an **aerobics** instructor at a local fitness centre.
- A **ward** is a room in a hospital with beds for patients.
- I try to **work out** at the gym at least twice a week.
- I hate injections! I feel faint if I just see a **syringe**!

1 The doctor said I had a chest infection and prescribed _____.
2 Fiona's got an appointment to see a _____ next month. She's hoping he'll know why she's been getting these terrible headaches.
3 If you want to get fit, maybe you should take up _____.
4 My grandfather's in a _____ with eighteen other patients.
5 When Karen's arm was _____, she had to learn to write with her left hand. She said it was very difficult.
6 The doctor said that, after the operation, I've got to keep my arm in a _____ for a couple of days.
7 I'd love to be able to _____ regularly, but I just can't find the time.
8 Medical treatment is free on the _____, but there are often long waiting lists for operations and appointments with consultants.
9 It's quite a deep cut. I don't think a _____ will be enough. You might need stitches.
10 The dentist used a _____ to anaesthetise my mouth before he started drilling.

Listening and Speaking Skills / Unit 12

Unit 12

EXAM PRACTICE — SPEAKING PARTS 3 AND 4

Exam know-how

When you do the Speaking Paper:
- Remember that it's better to use more complex grammar and sentence structures when you speak, even if you make mistakes. You gain marks for trying!
- Remember that you are not marked on your opinions and beliefs. However, you will lose marks if you what you say is not logical. Give sensible and logical reasons for your opinions.

A Part 3

I'd like you to imagine that you are responsible for putting together a first aid kit for your local youth club. Here are some things you might want to include.

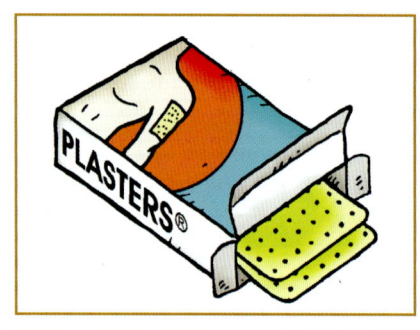

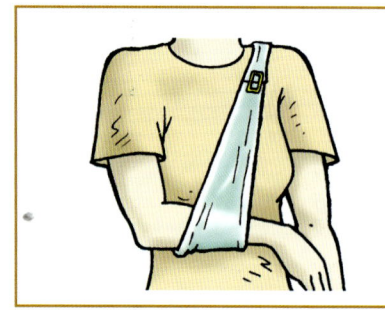

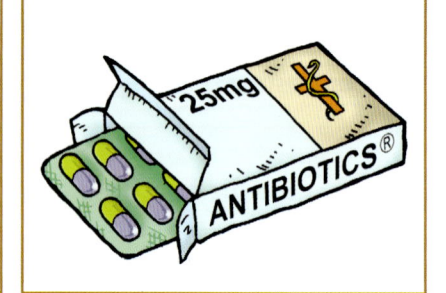

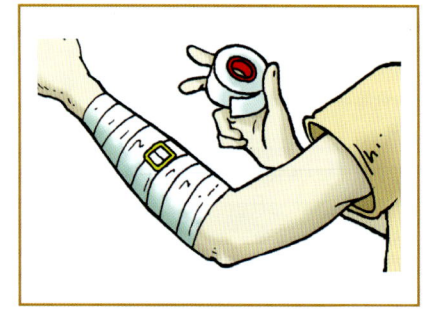

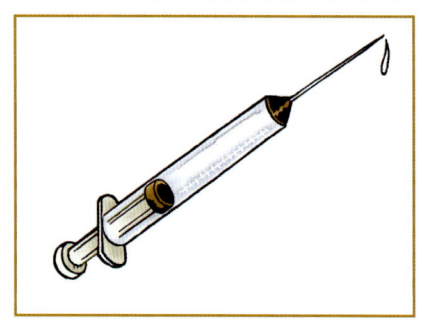

doctor 695949
hospital 474585
chemist 4838385
health centre 483828

3 min

I'd like you to talk to each other and discuss how useful these things are in a first aid kit. Then, I'd like you to decide which two things you would not include in the first aid kit for the youth club. Remember, you have about three minutes for this.

74

B Part 4

- Do you try to have a healthy diet?
- What are the best ways to stay fit and healthy?
- Do you exercise regularly?
- What is the health system like in your country?
- How do you feel when you go to the dentist?
- Can you think of any ways to improve the health system in your country?
- Would you like to work in the medical profession? Why/Why not?
- How important is it to know first aid?

Grammar focus

The gym **which** I go **to** is in the town centre.
The gym **where** I go is in the town centre.

'Where' can sometimes be used in place of 'to which', 'in which', 'at which' and 'from which'.

Write 'where' or 'which' in the gaps to complete the sentences.

1 Go to the chemist's _____ we got those bandages last week.
2 There are only six beds in the ward _____ my aunt is in.
3 The clinic _____ I went to is opposite the police station.
4 That's the health food shop _____ they sell loads of vegetarian products.
5 Have you heard of the Ipcress Diet? It's the one _____ you're allowed to eat lots of red meat.
6 She's going to go to the gym _____ she got the leaflets from last week.

Listening and Speaking Skills / Unit 12

Unit 13 Transport

WARM-UP — Pairwork

Look at the pictures. In pairs, answer the following questions:
- How dangerous are the roads where you live?
- How could they be made safer?
- How can children learn about road safety?

A

B

DEVELOP YOUR LISTENING SKILLS

A What's behind the words?

Listen to these extracts from comments on road safety by four people. Each speaker is concerned about a problem. Circle the problem they are probably talking about.

Speaker 1 is concerned about ...
a the cost of insurance.
b the speed of traffic.
c the condition of the road.

Speaker 2 is concerned about ...
a the amount of traffic.
b the lack of parking.
c the cost of petrol.

Speaker 3 is concerned about ...
a children's safety.
b traffic lights.
c roadworks.

Speaker 4 is concerned about ...
a drivers' skills.
b children's awareness.
c cars' facilities.

B Who's to blame?

Now listen to the complete comments.
Each speaker implies that somebody is to blame for the situation.
Match the speakers to the people they blame.
There is one extra letter you do not need to use.

Speaker 1 _____   A police
Speaker 2 _____   B car designers
Speaker 3 _____   C local council
Speaker 4 _____   D national government
                       E parents

C True or false?

Listen to the complete comments again.
Decide whether the following statements are true or false.
Circle **T** for True or **F** for False.

1 Speaker 1 thinks the problem could cause an accident.   **T / F**
2 Speaker 1 thinks the problem could take two years to fix.   **T / F**
3 Speaker 2 thinks the children should play somewhere else.   **T / F**
4 Speaker 2 accepted an apology from someone.   **T / F**
5 Speaker 3 thinks that the girl was fortunate.   **T / F**
6 Speaker 3's daughter is not allowed to play in the street.   **T / F**
7 Speaker 4 thinks that driving instructors don't drive safely.   **T / F**
8 Speaker 4 thinks the drivers should go a different way.   **T / F**

D Discuss

In pairs, check whether you agree on the answers to B and C.
Discuss why you chose those answers. If necessary, listen again.

Listening and Speaking Skills / Unit 13

Unit 13

DEVELOP YOUR LISTENING SKILLS

E Deduce the meaning
Listen to these statements taken from an advertisement for a new form of transport, the Solomobile. For each statement, choose the sentence below which best expresses what we can deduce about the Solomobile.

Statement 1
a The Solomobile uses another form of energy.
b The Solomobile uses less petrol than a car.

Statement 2
a The Solomobile doesn't run on wheels.
b The Solomobile doesn't need any brakes.

Statement 3
a The Solomobile is designed for this country.
b The Solomobile is new in this country.

F Listen and check
Now listen to the whole advertisement and check your answers to E.

Wordperfect

G What's being implied?

Listen again and decide what the advertisement implies about the following statements. Circle **T** for True and **F** for False.

1 Traffic jams are caused by people going too slowly. **T / F**

2 You'll have to pay for the energy the Solomobile uses. **T / F**

3 At the moment, we don't have complete freedom to travel. **T / F**

4 The Solomobile is designed for long journeys. **T / F**

5 People of different ages will find the Solomobile useful. **T / F**

H Discuss (Pairwork)

In pairs, discuss your answers to G. Did you agree about what was being implied? Explain why you chose your answers. What do you think of the idea of the Solomobile?

I Listen and discuss

Listen to the advertisement again. As you listen, decide whether you agree or disagree with the following statements. When you have listened, discuss your opinions. Give reasons.

1 We will have electric vehicles in the near future. **Agree / Disagree**

2 We will have vehicles that fly in the near future. **Agree / Disagree**

3 The Solomobile would be fun. **Agree / Disagree**

4 The Solomobile would replace cars. **Agree / Disagree**

5 Cars are the biggest threat to the environment. **Agree / Disagree**

Read these sentences and then use the words in bold to complete the sentences below.

- The **council** is the local government, usually responsible for roads, schools and local services.
- They're mending the road into town so we'll have to go another way to avoid the **roadworks**.
- I hope the car doesn't **break down** on the way to work like it did yesterday.
- We should take the **motorway** if we're going to drive so far.
- The government have started a major advertising campaign to deal with the problem of **drink-driving**.
- A **coach** is a large bus that usually runs between towns and cities.
- You have to stop and pay a **toll** on some major roads as a kind of tax.
- A **hydrofoil** is a passenger boat that goes quite fast and is lifted up by a kind of underwater wing.
- Let's take the **ferry** to the next island and spend a few days there.
- There's been an accident so the police have created a **diversion** onto another road and we have to turn left.

1 The train only runs twice a day, so I suggest we take the _____ and then get a taxi.

2 It might be more expensive than the ferry, but the _____ is much quicker.

3 Could you look in my bag to see if there's any money? We'll have to pay a _____ soon if we stay on this road.

4 Two people were injured earlier today in an accident on the _____ just outside Manchester.

5 If I _____ one more time, I'm selling this car and getting a new one.

6 There'll be delays on the M5 for the whole of next week due to _____.

7 We'll have to go the long way to Grandma's house as there's a _____ on the main road because of an accident.

8 The _____ might be slower than the hydrofoil, but it's certainly cheaper.

9 Did you hear about Darren's dad? He was arrested for _____ and might go to prison.

10 I think the local _____ is responsible for making sure the roads are in good condition.

Unit 13

EXAM PRACTICE — LISTENING PARTS 1 AND 2

Exam know-how

When you do Listening Part 1:
- Remember that the wrong answers are there for a reason. They are supposed to distract you so that you think they are right. Don't choose an answer just because you hear a word from the question.

When you do Listening Part 2:
- Read the whole sentence after you have written your answer. Does it make sense? The complete sentence should be grammatically correct, although you should write only the missing words on the answer sheet.

A Part 1

You will hear people talking in eight different situations. For questions **1-8**, choose the best answer, **A, B** or **C**.

1 You hear a young woman talking to her friend about a journey.
   What is her opinion of the driver?
   A He wasn't really prepared for the journey.
   B He didn't seem to care about the passengers.
   C He blamed somebody else for the problem.

2 You hear a man talking about his job. Where does he work?
   A on a ferry
   B at a port
   C in a travel agent's

3 You hear part of a radio programme on the subject of transport.
   What is the problem being discussed?
   A the pollution caused by cars
   B the lack of places to park
   C the danger of speeding motorists

4 Listen to this couple talking about a museum they are planning to visit.
   What do they disagree on?
   A how interesting it would be
   B how much time they will have there
   C how long it will take to get there

5 You overhear a woman talking to an air hostess. What does the woman want her to do?
   A speak to another passenger
   B help her with a piece of equipment
   C give something to her

6 Listen to this woman talking about a documentary she has just seen.
   What does she think about the programme?
   A It ignored the main problem.
   B It blamed the wrong people.
   C It used the wrong figures.

7 You overhear this man on his phone on the train.
   Where is the person he is speaking to?
   A in a car
   B at home
   C on a train

8 You hear part of a radio play. Why is the woman annoyed with the man?
   A He won't drive her somewhere.
   B He can't remember something.
   C He doesn't know how to do something.

80

B Part 2

You will hear a man being interviewed for an opinion survey about public transport. For questions **9-18**, fill in the questionnaire.

Public Transport Opinion Survey

Occupation? _____ 9
How often uses public transport? _____ 10
Any complaints? _____ 11
and _____ 12
Any positive aspects of service? _____ 13
and _____ 14

New Park and Ride Scheme
North car park   advantage: _____ 15
                  disadvantage: _____ 16
South car park   advantage: _____ 17
                  disadvantage: _____ 18

Grammar focus

Read these sentences and circle the correct words.

*'As I drove past, I **saw** Frances **crossing** the road, and then lost sight of her.'*
*'I **heard** two women **talking** about an accident on the bus but I had to get off at the next stop.'*

These people saw or heard all / part of the action they are talking about.

*'I'm sure Mary was on the ferry because I **saw** her **get on**.'*
*'I **heard** John **play** an Oasis song on his guitar and it was wonderful.'*

These people saw or heard all / part of the action they are talking about.

Complete the rule:

When **see** or **hear** are followed by _____, it usually means that the speaker only saw or heard part of an action.

When they are followed by _____, it usually means that the speaker say or heard all of the action.

Listen to these statements. For each one, decide whether the speaker saw or heard part or all of the action by circling the correct option.

Statement 1	Statement 2	Statement 3	Statement 4	Statement 5
a all	a all	a all	a all	a all
b part	b part	b part	b part	b part

Listening and Speaking Skills / Unit 13   81

Unit 14 Fashion

WARM-UP *Pairwork*

Look at the pictures. In pairs, answer the following questions:
- Would you like to work as a fashion designer? Why/Why not?
- Do you think clothes from the past can come back in fashion?
- How do you think fashion might change in the future?

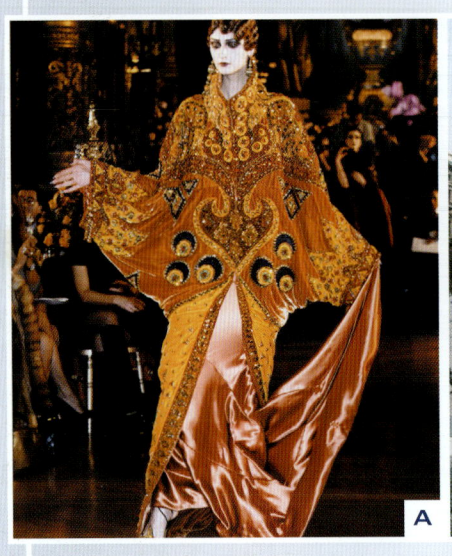

A   B   C

DEVELOP YOUR SPEAKING SKILLS

A Dos and Don'ts

Which of these are good things for you to say or do in the interview? Which of them are not so good? Write **Do** or **Don't** before each one.

1 _____ say everything in a voice that never goes up or down.
2 _____ let your voice rise and fall naturally.
3 _____ sound as if the interview is boring.
4 _____ sound as if the interview is interesting.
5 _____ speak clearly so that the others in the interview can hear you.
6 _____ mumble and cover your mouth with your hand.
7 _____ let your words flow naturally, with few hesitations.
8 _____ say '... erm ...' after every word.
9 _____ say anything in your first language.
10 _____ express yourself in English (even to the other candidate).

B How's it said?

Read the following passage and look at the phrases in bold. Decide how you would say them. Underline the syllable(s) you think you would stress.

'Some people have to always have the latest **CD player** or watch the latest **TV programme** or play the latest **video game**. Personally, I think there are a couple of **advantages and disadvantages** to being fashionable. **In my opinion**, spending a lot of money in **clothes shops** or **shoe shops** is usually a waste of money. **On the other hand**, sometimes it's worth buying good quality. **As far as I'm concerned**, people should just be themselves and not worry too much about fashion. **Anyway**, that's what I think.'

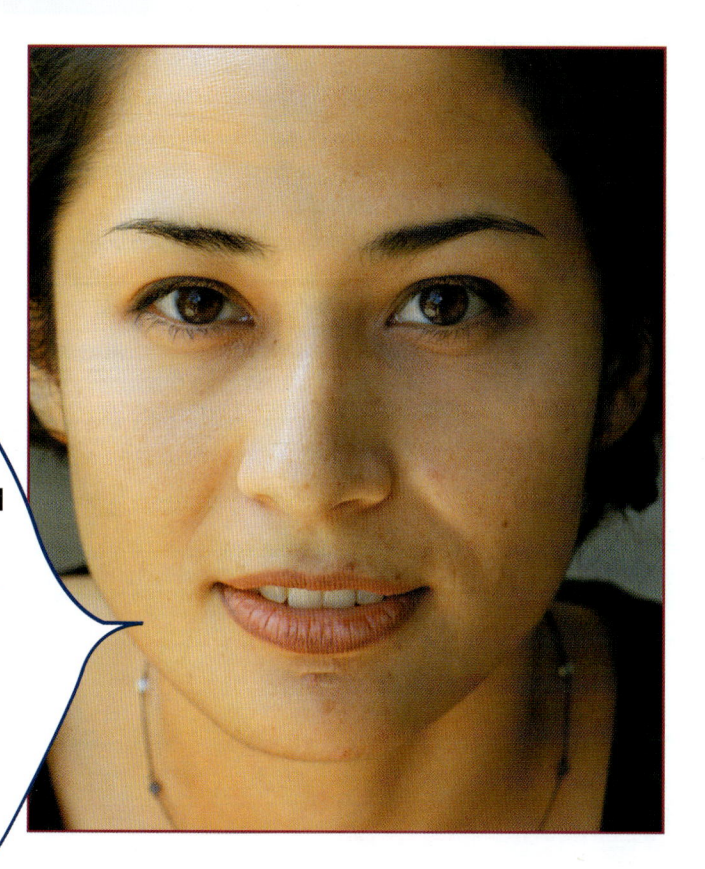

C Listen and check

Now listen to the person speaking and check your answers. When you have finished, compare your answers with your partner's. Did you agree about the way the phrases are pronounced?

D What do you think?

With your partner, take it in turns to ask and answer the following questions. Try to use the phrases from B and make sure that you stress them correctly.

1 How have video games changed recently?

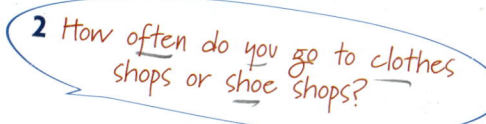

2 How often do you go to clothes shops or shoe shops?

3 What are the advantages and disadvantages of being fashionable?

4 Which TV programmes are popular at the moment?

Listening and Speaking Skills / Unit 14

Unit 14

DEVELOP YOUR SPEAKING SKILLS

E Which have the same sound?

In each line below, two of the words have the same vowel sound in them. Circle the two words. Say the words aloud to help you. Compare your answers with the rest of the class. Now check your answers by listening to the words.

1	heard	bear	beard	word
2	flood	broom	shut	lamp
3	were	wear	where	we're
4	term	warm	firm	farm
5	fur	fair	far	fir
6	flares	parents	hat	star
7	occur	air	appear	large
	ur	ai	ea	ar

F Find the silent letters

Look at these sentences. Each of them has at least one silent letter in it. Underline any letters which you think are not pronounced.

1 I've just got this new jacket and I can't fasten it.

2 I know it's fashionable, but if you wear that top you'll catch pneumonia.

3 Foreign clothes always seem to be so much better made.

4 The shop assistant had to climb a ladder to get the pair of shoes I wanted.

5 I'm really looking forward to the autumn fashions coming out.

6 Terry has started combing his hair in a more fashionable style.

G Listen and check

Listen to the sentences and check your answers. Compare your answers with your partner's.

Wordperfect

H Put it all together

Practise reading the following sentences with your partner. Listen to each other carefully to check for correct pronunciation. When you think you have got them right, read the sentences to the whole class. Now check by listening to the sentences.

1 As far as I'm concerned, following foreign fashions has its advantages and disadvantages.

2 My parents will be annoyed that I left my CD player in the clothes shop.

3 In my opinion, it's not fair to animals if people wear fur.

4 Anyway, what were you wearing when the incident occured?

5 On the other hand, if you shave, you don't have to comb your beard.

I Practise the tongue-twisters

In pairs, say the following sentences slowly and clearly. Then, try to say them faster and faster. Who can say them the fastest, without getting their tongue twisted?

Sam's shop stocks short spotted socks.

Red leather, yellow leather.

Which wristwatches are Swiss wristwatches?

Read these sentences and then use the words in bold to complete the sentences below.

- If clothes are **striped**, they have lines of different colours on them, like a zebra.
- If clothes are **checked**, they have squares of different colours on them, like a chessboard.
- I think it would be really **cool** to go to a fashion show and see the latest designs.
- If something is **out of date**, it is old-fashioned and probably useless.
- Teenagers feel **peer pressure** very strongly; they want to be like their friends and to do the same things as they do.
- You wear a **disguise** when you don't want other people to know who you are.
- Martha's wedding will be a great chance to **dress up** and wear our best clothes.
- This morning, I **put** my clothes **on** in a hurry and I've been wearing my pullover inside out all day!
- Do you like my new **outfit**? I got the trousers in the town centre, the shoes round the corner, and the top was a present.
- I'm sure the current fashion for nose rings is just a **fad**; it'll be gone before you know it.

1 The thief bought a wig to use as a _____ to escape from the police.

2 Many people first start smoking because of _____.

3 I _____ my T-shirt _____ the wrong way round and didn't notice.

4 I seem to see a lot of young people with dyed hair these days; I hope it's just a passing _____ because I don't really like it.

5 If you wear a _____ top, with the lines going vertically, it'll make you look taller.

6 If you're going to wear that black and white _____ shirt, make sure nobody tries to play chess on you!

7 I've bought a new hat and I'm looking forward to being able to _____ for the party next week.

8 I'm going to need a new _____ if we're going to dinner at your boss's house.

9 Most of my clothes seem to be _____; it's high time I got myself some new ones.

10 Doesn't Tracy look really _____ in her new outfit?

Listening and Speaking Skills / Unit 14

Unit 14

EXAM PRACTICE — SPEAKING PARTS 1 AND 2

Exam know-how

When you do the Speaking Paper:
- Don't worry too much about having an accent. The most important thing is that you can be understood easily, so speak as clearly and as naturally as you can. If your partner in the interview speaks in a way you don't understand, politely ask them to repeat what they have said.
- Remember that we usually stress 'I' or 'me' or 'my' when we are giving our opinion (As far as *I'm* concerned ..., If you ask *me* ..., In *my* opinion ...). Use these connecting phrases in the interview and try to stress them correctly.

A Part 1   3 MIN

We'd like to know something about you, so I'm going to ask you some questions about yourselves.

- What kind of clothes do you like to wear for special occasions?
- What kind of clothes do you like to wear?
- Do you keep up with current trends?
- Are you interested in fashion?
- Do you follow fashions in music?
- What was the last new item of clothing you bought?
- Do you like to dress up for special occasions?
- Do you like to get clothes as presents at Christmas or on your birthday?

B Part 2   1 MIN

Photos for Candidate A:

Candidate A, here are two photographs connected to clothes and fashion. I'd like you to compare and contrast them and say what aspects of the world of fashion they show. Remember, you only have one minute.

Candidate B, would you like to go to a fashion show?   20 SECS

86

Photos for Candidate B:

> Candidate B, here are two photographs of different kitchens. I'd like you to compare and contrast them and tell us which style of kitchen you would prefer to have in your home. Remember, you only have one minute.

> Candidate A, would you like to have a fashionable kitchen at home?

Grammar *focus*

Look at these sentences expressing negative ideas using 'thinking' verbs:

I **don't think** people care so much about fashion these days.
I **don't imagine** fashions will change that much in the future.
I **don't believe** anybody really wears the clothes they see at fashion shows.
I **don't suppose** designers consider ordinary people's needs.

Notice that the 'thinking' verb is made negative:

I don't think ..., I don't imagine ....

This is more natural than 'I think people don't care ...' **or** 'I imagine fashions won't change ...'.
Notice, though, that 'hope' is an exception.

I **hope** long hair **doesn't** come back into fashion.

Use the following prompts to write natural sentences in the negative. Make whatever changes are necessary.

1 Jenny / think / fashion be an interesting topic to write about
   _____

2 I / believe / jeans become unfashionable for a long time yet
   _____

3 Paul / hope / long jackets be in fashion again this year
   _____

4 I / can imagine / smoking ever be fashionable again
   _____

5 I / suppose / the shops have the latest styles in stock yet
   _____

Listening and Speaking Skills / Unit 14

Unit 15 Crime

WARM-UP *Pairwork*

Look at the pictures. In pairs, answer the following questions:
- Why do we have prisons?
- Do prisons work?
- What would be the worst thing about being in prison?
- What other ways of dealing with crime can you think of?

A

B

DEVELOP YOUR LISTENING SKILLS

A True or false?
Look at these statements about stress and intonation.
Decide whether each one is true or false. Circle **T** for True or **F** for False.

1 A speaker usually stresses the most important words.   **T / F**

2 Words like 'and', 'or' and 'of' are usually strongly stressed.   **T / F**

3 Stress is often used to show contrast with another word.   **T / F**

4 A speaker's voice usually doesn't go up or down much.   **T / F**

5 A speaker's intonation can tell us what answer they expect.   **T / F**

B Which words are stressed?

Read these sentences, which have been taken from longer comments on crime. Underline which word you think the speaker is going to stress most. Then listen and check your answers.

Speaker 1   I never thought the outside world would have changed so much.

Speaker 2   I did do what they said I'd done, but I'm sorry for it now.

Speaker 3   It's when they're on the outside that they have problems.

Speaker 4   When they caught the person who had done it, I was released.

C Choose the meaning

Listen to slightly longer extracts and decide which of the two options is true for each speaker. The words they stress will help you decide.

Speaker 1 uses stress to show ...
a how surprised he was by what happened.
b how sure he is about what happened.

Speaker 2 uses stress to show ...
a that he accepts that he was guilty.
b that he wasn't as bad as they thought.

Speaker 3 uses stress to contrast ...
a life in prison and life outside prison.
b criminals and ordinary people.

Speaker 4 uses stress to emphasize ...
a her anger.
b her innocence.

D Listen and match

Now listen to the complete comments. Match each speaker to one point they are making. There is one extra point you do not need to use.

Speaker 1 _____
Speaker 2 _____
Speaker 3 _____
Speaker 4 _____

A Prison can work as a deterrent.
B More training might help to prevent mistakes.
C Some people feel more secure in prison.
D More sports facilities for criminals might help.
E Putting criminals with other criminals is not a good idea.

Listening and Speaking Skills / Unit 15

Unit 15

DEVELOP YOUR LISTENING SKILLS

E What are they going to say?

Listen to these different people say the following words. Underline the word each speaker stresses and match each speaker to the words they are going to say.

Speaker 1
'If he shot the young man, ...
a why have they arrested Mrs Simpson?'
b why did he then stab the old man?'

Speaker 2
'If he shot the young man, ...
a why have they arrested Mrs Simpson?'
b why can't they find the gun?'

Speaker 3
'If he shot the young man, ...
a why can't they find the gun?'
b how did the old man die?'

Speaker 4
'If he shot the young man, ...
a why have they arrested Mrs Simpson?'
b why didn't he shoot the young woman?'

F Listen and check

Now listen to the speakers making the statements above and check your answers.

G Rising or falling?

Listen to these statements about crime. Listen to the intonation used by each speaker and decide whether their tone of voice is going up at the end (*rising*) or down at the end (*falling*).

Speaker 1   rising / falling

Speaker 2   rising / falling

Speaker 3   rising / falling

Speaker 4   rising / falling

Speaker 5   rising / falling

Wordperfect

H Listen and circle
Listen again and decide for each speaker whether the following statements are true or false. Circle **T** for True or **F** for False.

1 Speaker 1 isn't sure about the information. **T / F**

2 Speaker 2 is expecting the listener to agree. **T / F**

3 Speaker 3 isn't surprised by somebody's statement. **T / F**

4 Speaker 4 is sure that the statement is true. **T / F**

5 Speaker 5 is sure that the statement is true. **T / F**

I Practise your intonation
Pairwork

Look at the following sentences. With a partner, practise saying them with the correct intonation, falling if you are sure of the answer and rising if you aren't sure.

1 (not sure) You used to be in prison, didn't you?

2 (not sure) It's illegal to park here, isn't it?

3 (sure) You committed the crime, didn't you?

4 (sure) They should build more prisons, shouldn't they?

5 (not sure) You didn't do it, did you?

Read these sentences and then use the words in bold to complete the sentences below.

- A **court** is a place where a criminal trial takes place.
- My brother has a **criminal record** because of something he did wrong when he was younger.
- I've never been **in trouble** with the police, and I hope I never will.
- A **witness** claimed that she had seen the accused leaving the bank with the money.
- Old people are increasingly afraid of being **victims** of violent crime.
- A window had been smashed on the car where someone had tried to **break in**.
- The judge read the **verdict** in a steady voice: 'Guilty.'
- Because it was Ed's **first offence**, the judge let him off with just a warning.
- The burglar ran, but the police managed to **arrest** him before he got too far.
- The **justice system** has been criticised recently for a number of serious mistakes.

1 You aren't allowed to join the police force if you have a _____.
2 If you find yourself _____, make sure you call your lawyer immediately.
3 The robbers almost got away but a _____ in another house had written down the number of their car.
4 The police believe that the thieves managed to _____ through the back door.
5 Jane's really worried because her case comes up in _____ next Monday.
6 The police have announced that they are hoping to _____ somebody in connection with the crime very shortly.
7 The government has decided to completely change the _____ to make it fairer.
8 The accused woman lowered her head as the _____ was read out.
9 The punishment for your _____ is usually not as severe as it is for later crimes.
10 The _____ of the crime appeared on television to ask for help.

Listening and Speaking Skills / Unit 15 91

Unit 15

EXAM PRACTICE — LISTENING PARTS 3 AND 4

Exam know-how

When you do the Listening Paper:
- The words a speaker stresses can help you anticipate and understand what point they are making. We often stress words in English because we want to contrast that thing or idea with another thing or idea. In the exam, listen for words that are stressed. These are usually the words that carry the most information.

- In the exam, you are often asked to judge how a speaker feels or what their attitude is to what they are saying. Intonation and tone of voice can give you a lot of information about feelings and attitude. Listen to what they say, but also listen to how they say it.

A Part 3

You will hear five people talking about a prison. For questions **1-5**, choose which of the opinions **A-F** each speaker expresses. Use the letters only once. There is one extra letter you do not need to use.

A I hadn't expected the place to be like it is.

Speaker 1   [1]

B I think that more could be done with more money.

Speaker 2   [2]

C I don't believe prison does any good.

Speaker 3   [3]

D I believe that staff should be better trained.

Speaker 4   [4]

E I think criminals should be sent to prison more often.

Speaker 5   [5]

F I don't think the men work hard enough.

B Part 4

You will hear a radio interview with a man who used to be a criminal. For questions **6-12**, decide which views are expressed and which are not. In the boxes provided, write **YES** next to those views which are expressed and **NO** next to those views which are not expressed.

6	Prisons used to be much worse in the past.		6
7	Prisons teach you how to live a life away from crime.		7
8	Young people should study more to avoid a life of crime.		8
9	People might turn to crime when they feel hopeless.		9
10	Criminals are presented in a realistic way in the media.		10
11	People can be taught useful skills in prison.		11
12	Prisoners need more entertainment, such as sports on TV.		12

Grammar focus

Listen to these sentences being read and underline the stressed syllables in the words in blue.

None of the prisoners **object** to the new rules.
The prisoner was found carrying an illegal **object**.

When a noun and a verb are written in the same way, they are sometimes stressed the same. Sometimes, though, the stress gives you information about the part of speech.

Listen to these pairs of sentences.
Write the word which appears in both sentences and circle the correct answer.

1 The verb and noun are: _____.
   The verb is stressed on the first / second syllable and the noun is stressed on the first / second syllable.

2 The verb and noun are: _____.
   The verb is stressed on the first / second syllable and the noun is stressed on the first / second syllable.

3 The verb and noun are: _____.
   The verb is stressed on the first / second syllable and the noun is stressed on the first / second syllable.

4 The verb and noun are: _____.
   The verb is stressed on the first / second syllable and the noun is stressed on the first / second syllable.

What do you notice about each pair of words?

Unit 16 Shopping

WARM-UP Pairwork

Look at the pictures. Can you describe what is happening in each one?
Now, in pairs, suggest what you should do if:
- you buy a CD that won't play
- you find a hole in a sweater you've just bought
- you drop your new camera and it breaks
- two people buy you the same present for Christmas

DEVELOP YOUR SPEAKING SKILLS

A Dos and Don'ts

Which of these are good things for you to say or do in the interview?
Which of them are not so good? Write **Do** or **Don't** before each one.

1. _____ make reasonable suggestions to your partner.
2. _____ use the verb 'suggest' all the time.
3. _____ ignore your partner's suggestions and talk about other things.
4. _____ ask your partner questions about his or her suggestions.
5. _____ use your imagination to come up with good suggestions.
6. _____ use modals like 'could' and 'would' to make suggestions.
7. _____ use modals like 'must' and 'have to' to make suggestions.
8. _____ explain why you are recommending something.

B How do they suggest it?

Listen to the following extracts taken from different interviews with students. For each student, choose the phrase you hear them use to make a suggestion or recommendation. What do you think each student is talking about?

Student 1
a Don't you think that …
b Would you think that …

Student 2
a I recommend that …
b I recommend her that …

Student 3
a She ought to …
b She might do …

Student 4
a I will suggest …
b I suggest …

Student 5
a What do you think …
b What would you think …

Student 6
a One thing she could do is …
b One thing she would do is …

C Complete the suggestions

Complete the following suggestions and recommendations using some of the phrases in the box. There may be more than one answer. Then, decide whether each one is formal or informal by circling the correct option.

> Do you think it would be a good idea to …
> I would say that …
> I/I'd I would like to suggest …
> What about …
> My recommendation would be to …
> How about …
> One possibility is that …
> Couldn't we …
> Why don't we …

1 _____ try taking the CD back to the shop we bought it from?   **formal / informal**

2 _____ the best idea is probably to send it back to the manufacturer.   **formal / informal**

3 _____ checking that it's still under guarantee?   **formal / informal**

4 _____ we could write a letter of complaint to the shop.   **formal / informal**

5 _____ ask the shop for our money back.   **formal / informal**

6 _____ there's actually very little you can do.   **formal / informal**

7 _____ phoning the shop to see what they say.   **formal / informal**

Unit 16

DEVELOP YOUR SPEAKING SKILLS

D What do you suggest? *Pairwork*

What would you say to the following people if they asked you for advice? In pairs, decide on suggestions you could make using the phrases in B and C. Discuss your ideas with the class. Think about how formal your language should be.

1 a friend, who doesn't like shopping in large stores

2 your teacher, who wants to find a place that sells computers

3 your mum, who has a complaint about a shop assistant

4 a shop owner you work for, who wants to attract more customers

E Discuss

In pairs, imagine one of you has bought one of these items and discovered a problem with it. Decide which item you have bought and what the problem is. Discuss what you could do about the problem. Use the ways of making suggestions given in B and C.

F Roleplay

Imagine you have decided to take your item back to the place where you bought it. One of you is the customer and the other is the manager of the store. Roleplay the conversation they have, using good ways of making suggestions. Some of you might like to perform your roleplays for the whole class. You can start like this:

'Hello. I'd like to speak to the manager about this _____ I bought here.'

'Of course. I'm the manager. What seems to be the problem?'

- explain what the problem is
- suggest what the customer could do
- explain why that's not possible, or describe another problem

Wordperfect

Read these sentences and then use the words in bold to complete the sentences below.

- If you go **window shopping**, you look at what's in the shops but you don't buy anything.
- Please pay for your items at the nearest **checkout** as the store is closing in ten minutes.
- In Britain, people buy newspapers, cigarettes and sweets at a **newsagent's**.
- I got these shoes off a **market stall**, so they were quite cheap.
- An **aisle** is a row of shelves in a supermarket where you take what you want and put it in your trolley.
- If something is **on offer**, the price is lower than it usually is.
- Why don't you pay for your car in monthly **instalments** so that you don't have to spend all that money at once?
- At a **charity shop** you find second-hand things at a cheap price. The money you spend goes to charity.
- Only 400 euros for a brand-new computer? That's a real **bargain**!
- You shouldn't buy food if it's after the **sell-by date** that's written on the packet.

1 You'll find the toiletries in the next _____, next to the baby food.
2 These shoes were a _____. I only paid ten euros for them.
3 I haven't got any money this week, but we could go _____ if you like.
4 The problem with buying things from a _____ is that you can never find them again if something is wrong.
5 It seems a bit expensive, but perhaps I can afford it if I pay in _____.
6 Excuse me, but did you know that this cheese you're selling has a _____ of five days ago on it?
7 I like to buy something from the _____, even if I don't need it. The money all goes to help people.
8 There was such a long queue at the _____ that I put the things back and left the shop.
9 We would like to inform all our customers that most of our fruit and vegetables are _____ all this week.
10 I'm just going to pop to the _____ for a paper and a drink.

Listening and Speaking Skills / Unit 16

Unit 16

EXAM PRACTICE — SPEAKING PARTS 3 AND 4

Exam know-how

In Speaking Part 3:
- One of the things you are marked on is how well you interact with your partner. A good way to keep the conversation going is to make suggestions in the form of questions. If you say, 'What about ...?' or 'Couldn't we ...?', your partner has to respond to your suggestion. The examiner will notice how you used your suggestion and give you credit for it.

- If you don't understand what your partner is suggesting, don't just say 'I agree' and ignore it. Ask them to explain what they mean. You don't lose marks for asking them to make it clearer – you gain marks for good interaction.

A Part 3

> I'd like you to imagine that a large shopping centre is going to be built in your local area. Here are some of the shops and facilities they are thinking of having. Talk to each other about how popular you think these shops and facilities would be and then decide which two you think should not be included. Remember, you have about three minutes for this.

3 min

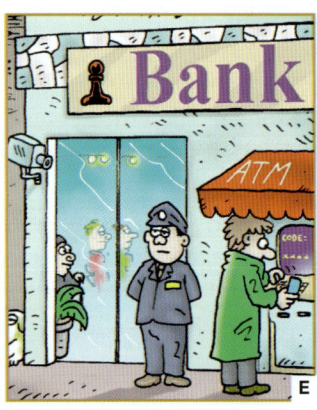

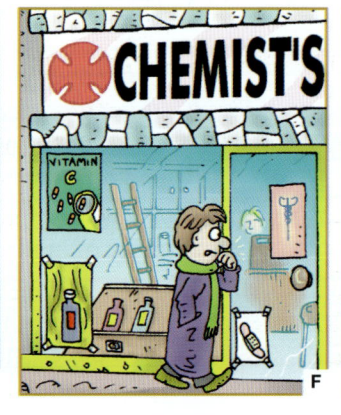

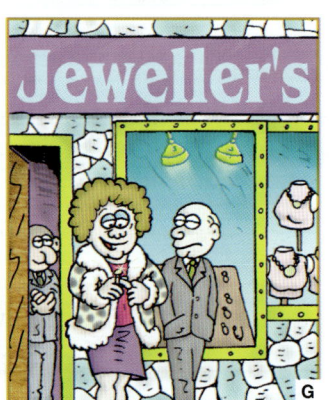

B Part 4

- What other kinds of shops would you like to see in it?
- Would this kind of shopping centre be popular in your area?
- Do you think some people spend too much time shopping?
- How do you think shopping will change in the future?
- Do you think large supermarkets are a threat to small shops?
- Are there any special things for tourists to buy in your area?
- Do you think you would enjoy running a shop?

Grammar focus

Look at these sentences:
That's a good idea, but **what if** we also spoke to the manager?
Suppose we ring the shop. What do you think they'll say?

These two structures can be used to make suggestions and raise possibilities. They can be used with a verb in the present or the past. A verb in the present makes the suggestion sound more certain.

Rewrite the following suggestions using the word or phrase given. Use a verb in the past tense.

1 We could drive to the shopping centre and have a look around. (**what if**)
   _____

2 We might suggest that she get a part-time job in a shop. (**suppose**)
   _____

3 I suggest we get the bus into town and meet outside the shopping centre. (**what if**)
   _____

4 I would like to suggest not including the bank and the bookshop in the shopping centre. (**suppose**)
   _____

5 My recommendation would be to contact the person in charge. (**what if**)
   _____

Listening and Speaking Skills / Unit 16

Exam *know-how*

The interview is your chance to show how good your spoken English is. Remember that it lasts approximately fourteen minutes and there are usually two candidates and two examiners.

How to do ... Speaking Part 1

1 UCLES will send you a timetable telling you when and where your interview is. Your teacher will tell you where you have to go and what you have to do.

2 When the time for your interview comes, the local supervisor will ask you to wait outside the room. If the other candidate is someone you don't know, this might be a good chance to say a quick hello and find out their name so that you can use it in the interview.

3 This is also a good time to get rid of any chewing gum. You can't produce your best English if you have something in your mouth!

4 Wait until one of the examiners asks you to come in. Go into the room and smile and say 'Hi.' or 'Hello.' or 'Good morning/afternoon.' to the examiners. (Do not say 'Goodbye'!) Sit down when the examiner asks you to and hand over your mark sheets.

5 The examiner will introduce him/herself and the assessor and ask for your names. They want to know your first name, so instead of answering 'Adams Nicola', simply say 'Nicola' or 'Nicky'.

6 You will be asked a few questions about yourself, your hobbies, etc. Listen to the questions and answer clearly. Try to relax. Forget about the assessor.

7 This part of the interview is designed to help you feel more comfortable. If you are nervous, take a deep breath and smile before continuing.

How to do ... Speaking Part 2

Your turn:

1 The examiner will give you two photographs. Look at the photographs and listen to the question. You will be asked to compare and contrast the photographs and express an opinion. Listen carefully to the second half of the question so you know what you are being asked to do.

2 Compare and contrast the photographs and express the opinion you have been asked for. Do not describe the photographs in detail.

3 If you do mention something in a photo, try not to say, 'I can see ...'. Say, 'There is / There are ...'.

4 Use good discursive words and phrases, such as 'On the one hand ... on the other hand ...' or '... whereas ...'.

5 Make sure you speak for one minute. Don't worry if the examiner interrupts you. They have to do that so there is time for the whole interview. It does not mean you have done anything wrong.

Your partner's turn:

1 Look at the photographs your partner is given and listen to the question they have been asked.

2 While your partner is talking, listen to what they are saying. If you are asked whether you agree or not, you should know what they said!

3 After one minute, your partner will stop and the examiner will ask you a follow-up question. This is usually something like 'Which one would you prefer?' or 'Do you like ...?'

4 You only need to give a short answer here. Don't worry if the examiner stops you saying too much.

How to do ... Speaking Part 3

1 The examiner will ask you to speak to your partner and give you a task to do together. Listen carefully to the question. You are often asked to imagine a situation. Usually, you are asked to do **two** things in the task. Remember to do both of them.

2 If you are not sure what you have to do, ask the examiner to repeat the instructions. Say: 'I'm sorry. Do you think you could explain it again, please?'

3 When you start, don't talk to or look at the examiner. Talk to and look at your partner.

4 Don't expect your partner to begin. A good way to start is by asking your partner a question using a phrase like 'Do you think ...?'

5 Remember it is supposed to be a conversation. Make one point and then ask your partner for their opinion.

6 Use all the good phrases you know for making suggestions and recommendations and for agreeing and disagreeing with your partner.

7 Remember what you have been asked to do. If you have been asked to choose two or three of the pictures, don't forget to do it.

8 Make sure you speak for about three minutes. Don't worry if the examiner interrupts you. They have to do that so there is time for the whole interview.

How to do ... Speaking Part 4

1 The examiner will ask you and your partner some questions about the theme of Part 3. Listen and make sure you answer the question.

2 Listen to what your partner says. It is a good idea to look at your partner while they are talking.

3 Don't speak only to the examiner. It is supposed to be a discussion between the three of you. Say to your partner things like 'I agree with you, and ...' or 'What you said is right, and I think ...'.

4 The examiner will tell you that the test is over. Do not ask if you have passed because they cannot tell you.

5 Say 'Bye.' or 'Goodbye.' or 'Nice to have met you.' and leave the interview room. Do not say 'Hello'!

Useful Phrases for Paper 5 – Speaking

Here are some expressions and phrases you can use in the Speaking paper. Remember that you can use some of them in more than one part of the interview. See the relevant speaking units for more useful phrases.

Greetings and farewells
Hi.
Hello. Pleased to meet you.
Good morning.
Good afternoon.
Bye.
Goodbye.
Nice to have met you.

Part 1
There are (four, etc) of us in my family.
I've lived here all my life, and …
I've been living here / studying English for (seven, etc) years.
I go to a comprehensive / secondary school in …
I'm in the (third, etc) year.
One of my favourite subjects is … (Chemistry, etc).
I'm at university, studying … (Physics, Medicine, etc).
We both go to the same language school / English school.
I haven't really decided yet, but …
One ambition of mine is to …
Although I don't have much free time, I like …
When I can, I like …

Part 2
To begin with, …
This is a photograph of …
In the picture, there's a …
The first point I'd like to make is …
Another similarity is …
Similarly, …
On the one hand, …
On the other hand, …
… whereas …
… while …
In contrast, …
However, …
I can't quite make out …
I can't really tell …
To be honest, I'm not sure …
As for which I would prefer, …
Personally, …
As far as I'm concerned, …
In my opinion, …

Part 3
I'm sorry. Do you think you could explain it again, please?
I'm sorry. I didn't catch what you said.
What do you think about …?
How about …?
I'd like to suggest …
One possibility is …
Absolutely.
I completely agree, and …
In a way, you are right.
I partly agree with you, but …
I agree to a certain extent, but …
That's a good point, and …
I'm afraid I don't agree because …
I have to disagree. Don't you think …?
So, which do you think we should choose?
If you ask me, …
To sum up, then, we've chosen …

Part 4
As I said earlier, I think …
That's a good question. I suppose …
As you said, (Mary), there's …
To my mind, …
As far as I'm concerned, …
To be honest, I'm not sure, but …
Personally, …
I've never really thought about that, but …
Well, that's an interesting question, but …

Speaking exam practice 1

Part 1 3 min

Your teacher will ask you a few questions about yourself.

Part 2 4 min

Photos for Candidate A:

Photos for Candidate B:

Listening and Speaking Skills / Exam practice

PART 3   3 min

PART 4   4 min

Your teacher will ask you some questions related to the theme of Part 3.

Speaking exam practice 2

Part 1 3 min

Your teacher will ask you a few questions about yourself.

Part 2 4 min

Photos for Candidate A:

Photos for Candidate B:

Listening and Speaking Skills / Exam practice

PART 3   3 min

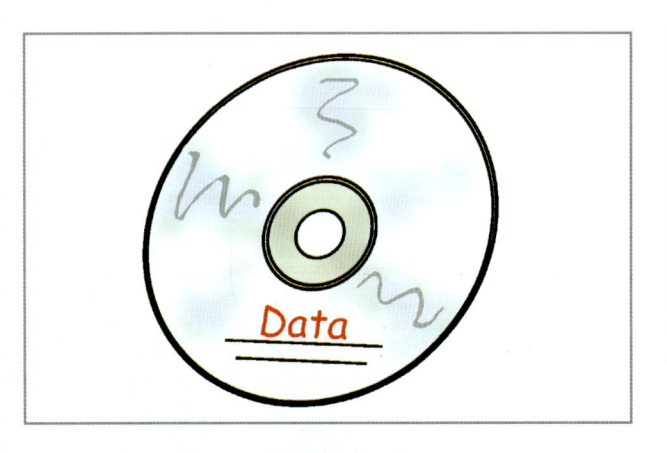

PART 4   4 min

Your teacher will ask you some questions related to the theme of Part 3.

Speaking exam practice 3

Part 1 3 min

Your teacher will ask you a few questions about yourself.

Part 2 4 min

Photos for Candidate A:

Photos for Candidate B:

PART 3   3 MIN

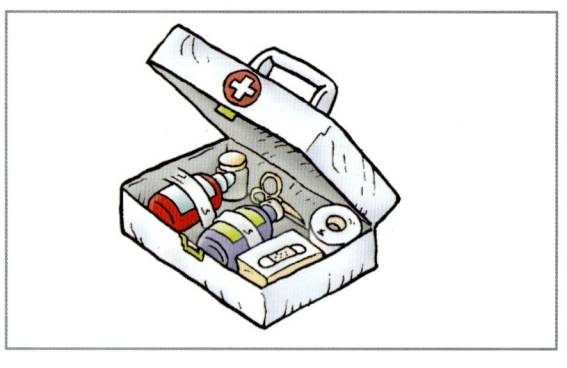

PART 4   4 MIN

Your teacher will ask you some questions related to the theme of Part 3.

108

LISTENING SKILLS DEVELOPMENT – SPECIFIC INFORMATION

Listen to these sentences. For each question, circle the correct answer.

1. How long did it take?
   a 15 minutes
   b 45 minutes
   c an hour

2. How many people will there be in total?
   a 14
   b 17
   c 19

3. How much did it cost?
   a 65 euros
   b 45 euros
   c 20 euros

4. How is the name spelt?
   a Thomson
   b Tompson
   c Thompson

5. What's the phone number?
   a 9122573
   b 9122753
   c 9211753

6. Which model did the speaker buy?
   a SX-120
   b XS-210
   c XS-21

7. Which two things are mentioned?
   a a CD and a cake
   b a CD and a tape
   c a CD-ROM and a tape

8. What is the person talking about?
   a rings
   b earrings
   c nose rings

9. What is the frequency of the radio station?
   a 89.8 FM
   b 98.9 FM
   c 99.8 FM

10. What time does the plane take off?
    a 6.45
    b 7.15
    c 7.45

11. Which flight is it?
    a OA903
    b OA9312
    c OA9031

12. What are the directions?
    a go straight on
    b turn left
    c turn right

13. How much does the woman have to pay?
    a £48
    b £48-£50
    c £48.50

14. How far is it?
    a 4km
    b 14km
    c 40km

15. How old will she be?
    a 19
    b 90
    c 96

Listening and Speaking Skills / Skills development 109

LISTENING SKILLS DEVELOPMENT – ATTITUDE AND OPINION

Listen to these sentences. For each question, circle the correct option to complete the sentence.

1. The speaker is _____.
   a disbelieving
   b annoyed
   c furious

2. The speaker is _____.
   a uncertain
   b surprised
   c expecting the answer, 'No.'

3. The speaker is _____.
   a uncertain
   b surprised
   c expecting the answer, 'No.'

4. The speaker is _____.
   a nervous
   b angry
   c upset

5. The speaker is _____.
   a agreeing completely
   b partly disagreeing
   c completely disagreeing

6. The speaker thinks that getting the tickets _____.
   a can't be difficult
   b was difficult
   c will be difficult

7. The speaker is _____.
   a depressed
   b disappointed
   c pessimistic

8. The speaker is _____.
   a modest
   b boastful
   c shy

9. The speaker is _____.
   a polite
   b kind
   c impolite

10. The speaker _____.
    a asks a question
    b gives a command
    c makes a suggestion

11. The speaker is _____.
    a hopeful
    b regretful
    c hopeless

12. The speaker is _____.
    a being sarcastic
    b giving a command
    c expressing certainty

13. The speaker is _____.
    a asking for advice
    b disagreeing
    c making a suggestion

14. The speaker _____.
    a feels insulted
    b does not feel insulted
    c never feels insulted

15. The speaker is _____.
    a expressing a concern
    b giving an opinion
    c revealing a secret

UNIVERSITY of CAMBRIDGE
ESOL Examinations

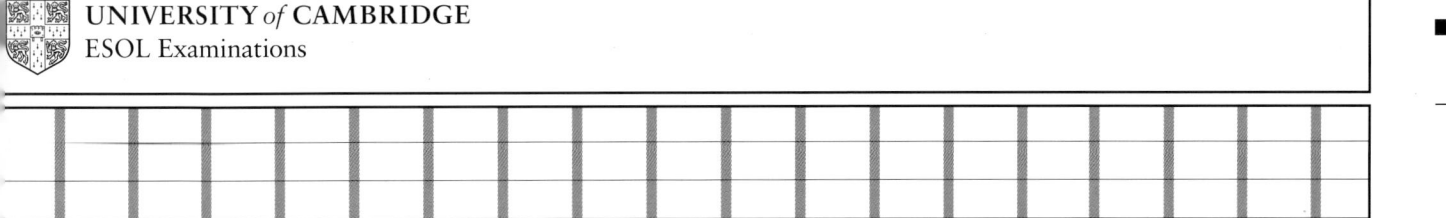

Candidate Name
If not already printed, write name in CAPITALS and complete the Candidate No. grid (in pencil).

Candidate Signature

Examination Title

Centre

Supervisor:
If the candidate is ABSENT or has WITHDRAWN shade here

Centre No.

Candidate No.

Examination Details

SAMPLE

Candidate Answer Sheet: FCE Paper 4 Listening

Mark test version (in PENCIL)
A B C D E
Special arrangements S H

Instructions

Use a PENCIL
Rub out any answer you wish to change using an eraser.

For **Parts 1** and **3**:
Mark ONE letter for each question.

For example, if you think **B** is the right answer to the question, mark your answer sheet like this:

0 A B C

For **Parts 2** and **4**:
Write your answers in the spaces next to the numbers like this:

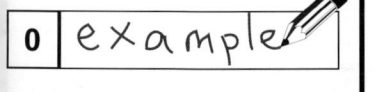

0 example

Part 1
1 A B C
2 A B C
3 A B C
4 A B C
5 A B C
6 A B C
7 A B C
8 A B C

Part 2
		Do not write here
9		1 9 0
10		1 10 0
11		1 11 0
12		1 12 0
13		1 13 0
14		1 14 0
15		1 15 0
16		1 16 0
17		1 17 0
18		1 18 0

Part 3
19 A B C D E F
20 A B C D E F
21 A B C D E F
22 A B C D E F
23 A B C D E F

Part 4
		Do not write here
24		1 24 0
25		1 25 0
26		1 26 0
27		1 27 0
28		1 28 0
29		1 29 0
30		1 30 0

FCE 4   DP320/094

Reproduced by permission of the University of Cambridge Local Examinations Syndicate.